# PHOTOGRAPHING
# Garden Wildlife

# PHOTOGRAPHING
# Garden Wildlife

Marianne Taylor and Steve Young

NEW HOLLAND

First published in 2009 by New Holland Publishers
London ● Cape Town ● Sydney ● Auckland
www.newhollandpublishers.com

Garfield House, 86-88 Edgware Road, London W2 2EA, United Kingdom
80 McKenzie Street, Cape Town, 8001, South Africa
Unit 1, 66 Gibbes Street, Chatswood, NSW 2067, Australia
218 Lake Road, Northcote, Auckland, New Zealand

Publisher: Simon Papps
Editor: Roy Woodward
Designer: Neal Cobourne
Production: Melanie Dowland
Publishing Director: Rosemary Wilkinson

Reproduction by Pica Digital (Pte) Ltd, Singapore
Printed and bound in Singapore by Tien Wah Press

All images by Steve Young except the following:

Robert Cardell: pages 14, 18, 24 (left), 29, 41 (left), 42-43, 67 (below), 85 (below), 93, 110, 116, 117 (right)
Kevin Keatley/ Wildlife-watching Supplies: page 41 (right)
Nikon: pages 49 and 55
Panasonic: page 51 (below)
Marianne Taylor: pages 24-25 (centre), 25 (right), 28, 30, 31, 32, 34, 40 (both), 45 (above),
58-59, 63 (above), 80-81, 85 (above), 89, 98, 99, 112, 114, 115, 117 (left)

# Contents

# Introduction

It is a paradox, but in some ways the digital age has brought us closer to the natural world than ever before. We can watch high-definition wildlife dramas filmed from Svalbard to the Serengeti on wall-sized TVs, we can carry the song of a Nightingale around on our mobile phones, and we can go online and look through a live webcam into a nest of wild Ospreys – witnessing everything from the moment the eggs hatch to the chicks' first flight. All of this is enough to inspire anyone to pick up a digital camera and head for the great outdoors.

**Blackbird on ivy**
This image was taken in the back yard shown opposite; the pair of Blackbirds always left by the same route, going on to the ivy-covered wall before flying away. By using the back bedroom window as a hide it was just a matter of waiting for the birds to land after they had finished feeding. Taking this shot on a snowy day was an added bonus.
*Nikon D2X, Sigma 300-800mm lens (at 340mm), ISO 400, 1/40th sec at f5.6*

However, as seasoned wildlife watchers know, and everyone else suspects, the outdoors is not always so great when it comes to finding wildlife. You set out for a walk in the country, hoping to see, and photograph, all sorts of wild creatures, but things do not always go according to plan. There may not be as much wildlife around as you'd like. What's more, when you do encounter a subject it rarely cooperates. Birds fly away, butterflies refuse to keep still, and mammals stay in hiding, leaving you to puzzle over their footprints, burrows and the discarded remains of their lunch. Real photo opportunities are as brief as they are infrequent – often you have just a few seconds to capture the shot before the animal realizes what's happening and makes a run for it. Finally, the camera doesn't always behave as you think it's going to.

Of course, whether you come home from your walk with a bushel of stunning images, or a handful of greyish blurs, depends a great deal on where you go, and when, as well as how much time you spend there and what kind of camera you have. However, perhaps the most important factor is experience – how well you know your camera, and how well you know the animals at which you're pointing it. To gain that all-important experience, and to enjoy and photograph some great wildlife encounters in their own right, look no further than your own back yard.

# The garden

In a landscape increasingly dominated by concrete and monoculture, Britain's gardens constitute an ever more vital wildlife habitat. For animals, gardens don't exist in isolation – they connect up to form often sizeable patches of what is effectively a mosaic of woodland, meadow and scrubland. You may be surprised to learn how many different species of animal and plant are forging a living in yours.

**Back yard**

It may not look much, but this small area can be a haven for wildlife. The feeders and apples attract birds such as Blue Tit, Blackbird, Woodpigeon, House Sparrow and Goldfinch. Add other wildlife such as Red Admiral, Comma and Holly Blue butterflies and other invertebrates and there are enough subjects in this tiny area for many photographic studies.
*Nikon D300, Sigma 18-50mm lens (at 18mm), ISO 400, 1/30th sec at f5.6*

If you're an aspiring wildlife photographer, the great thing about your garden is the control that you have over it. Not only can you boost its attractiveness to wildlife in general, and (within reason) to particular species, but you can also set the scene so that when the star visitor arrives, it steps onto a ready-made photography set and capturing the perfect image is just a formality. Best of all, you can explore the potential of this doorstep studio whenever you like.

This book sets out to help you discover, and get familiar with, the natural world in your garden, to find ways to make it more appealing to a greater variety of mammals, birds, insects and other wild animals, and to set up and capture rewarding photographs of those creatures and their environment. In doing so, you'll enhance your photography skills, learn a great deal about what makes our wild animals tick and discover how to make a wildlife haven in your own little corner of the great outdoors.

**House Sparrow male**
This was taken from the same bedroom window as the Blackbird image on page 6. After the House Sparrows had finished feeding, they regularly used the buddleia bush growing wild on a neighbour's wall as a perch before flying away.
*Nikon D2X, Sigma 300-800mm lens (at 650mm), ISO 200, 1/80th sec at f5.6*

# CHAPTER 1 What lives in your garden

**Goldfinch**

You don't have to own a large garden or country estate to attract Goldfinches; seed feeders, especially ones with nyjer seed, will entice them, or leave a patch of garden to grow wild with weeds as they love to feed on the natural seeds.

*Nikon D300, Nikkor 500mm f4 lens, ISO 320, 1/160th sec at f5.6*

If you live in the Fens, you'll have a different set of animals using your garden than someone who lives on Dartmoor, and the average Surrey bird table will draw a different crowd from one in an Orkney back yard. There will also be seasonal variations and some gardens will, by virtue of their location, pick up more 'passing trade' in the way of nomadic species, while others will have a higher proportion of resident wildlife. However, there are broad similarities that hold true across most of the British Isles. The guide below takes a look at the likely typical fauna of a typical garden.

### Mammals

Next door's cat aside, most mammals are not obvious garden visitors as they are secretive by nature and only really active at night. One exception is the Grey Squirrel. Unpopular in many quarters, for lots of good reasons, this is nonetheless an attractive, entertaining and photogenic animal. If your garden is 'south of the border' and has any kind of mature trees in its immediate vicinity, you probably see Grey Squirrels all the time.

If you live on the Isle of Wight, or in certain parts of Cumbria, Northumberland or rural Scotland, you may be lucky enough to have Red Squirrels in your garden. Like the Greys, they are active in the daytime and no slouches at exploiting food put out for the birds, so if they are there they are often easy to see.

If you've ever woken up on bin-day to behold your wheelie bin overturned, and your black sacks torn open and the contents strewn liberally across your garden, you may take a rather dim view of the remarkably resourceful urban Red Fox. Those who've had chickens or pet rabbits killed by foxes will be even less enchanted, but foxes have many fans by virtue of their beauty, character and charisma. The only predatory mammal likely to be seen in most gardens, foxes travel widely and exploit all kinds of food sources. They are also smart enough to quickly become accustomed to people, in the right circumstances, although their nocturnal habits present a challenge to the photographer.

**Grey Squirrel close-up**
If your garden is near a park or woodland it will probably be visited by Grey Squirrels. Much disliked they may be, but there is no doubt that they do make a good photographic subject.
*Nikon D2X, Sigma 300-800mm lens (at 700mm), ISO 200, 1/400th sec at f10*

Even small gardens are likely to be used by various small rodents. The Brown Rat and House Mouse are closely associated with human habitation – there's every chance they visit your garden already. More appealing to most are their rural relatives – the Wood Mouse, the larger Yellow-necked Mouse (southern England only), the Bank Vole and the Short-tailed Vole. These rodents need a reasonable amount of cover and plenty of natural food. They are far from obvious garden inhabitants, but with cunning, patience and a supply of nuts, seeds and other tasty bait you should be able to see and photograph them. Common Shrews and Pygmy Shrews are also widespread and present in many rural gardens – you might have heard them squeaking furiously as they rocket about in the undergrowth – but because they eat insects and other small animals, they are less easy to bait than the rodents.

Most British gardens will be hawked over in summer by at least one species of bat. The likeliest contenders are the Noctule (if it's big) and the Common Pipistrelle (if it's small), but rural gardens could attract many more. Often easy to see – or perhaps easy to glimpse – bats are far from easy to photograph well, but they often patrol the same area for lengthy spells, providing plenty of opportunities for practice.

Larger country gardens may attract a wider range of exciting mammalian visitors. Badgers are often common in wooded areas and will come for food put out for them; the same is true of Hedgehogs. Keeping Badgers from digging up the lawn is sometimes more of a challenge than attracting them in the first place. Deer, especially Roe Deer and the introduced Muntjac, may also become regular visitors if they can gain access and find something delicious to browse on in your garden, ditto Rabbits.

Any other mammalian visitors encountered in the average garden are likely to be there by accident rather than design. I have seen Weasels, Stoats and, once, even an Otter in modest-sized country gardens, but these were one-off visitations. Even so, the richer your garden is in wildlife species generally, the greater the chances of something out of the ordinary deciding to drop by.

**Wood Mouse**
They're probably more noticeable if they get inside the house, but mice will visit bird tables to hunt for food, or pick spilt seed from the ground as this one is doing.
*Nikon D2X, Sigma 300-800mm lens (at 800mm), ISO 200, 1/200th sec at f5.6*

# Bat detective

Our ability to detect high-frequency sounds deteriorates with age, unfortunately. However, if you are under 30 and haven't attended too many rock concerts, you may well be able to hear the high-pitched squeaks bats make (especially the bigger species, with their deeper voices) as they fly around searching for moths and other prey. They explore their environment by sound, squeaking and listening for the echo of the squeak as it bounces off an object. If the echo comes from a big, solid object, the bat knows not to fly into it. If the object is small and moving, it may be lunch and the bat will swoop in to investigate,

squeaking all the while to get more information. Try tossing a tiny pebble high in the air in the vicinity of a hunting bat – it may well dive down in pursuit of it before realizing it's not something edible. (Don't do this too often though. It's probably extremely annoying for the bat.)

You can find out which bats are using your garden by using a bat detector. These small, portable devices make bats' sounds audible to humans and help to separate the different frequencies of the various bat species' squeaks – so you can find and identify them whether you can hear them yourself or not. They may not help you with your photography, but they will certainly let you know what's about and when.

## Birds

Britain's garden birds, in all their variety and beauty, have inspired a thriving industry. We spend a small fortune feeding them and providing them with living quarters, and derive hours of pleasure from watching them. For a great many of us, it is the birdlife of our garden that inspires us to reach for the camera.

Because most birds can, and do, travel freely, almost any British species could potentially be seen in, or at least over, your garden. Many dedicated birders keep a 'garden list' and those who live in particularly good spots (especially on the coast) may amass 100 or more species, but many of these will be one-off 'fly-overs'. Typical garden birds amount to a rather more manageable number.

**Dunnock**
Dunnocks spend a lot of time grovelling about on the ground, making photography a challenge, but look (and listen) out for males giving their pleasant warbling song from higher perches. *Panasonic DMC-FZ18, ISO 100, 1/500th sec at f4.2*

Blue Tits and Great Tits are regular visitors to virtually every garden in mainland Britain. They can be attracted to window feeders even in the heart of central London. They are quick to discover new bird feeders, and their colourful plumage, boldness and acrobatic antics make them ideal subjects for the beginner to wildlife photography. Coal and Long-tailed Tits are also common garden birds. The rest of the group; Marsh, Willow and Crested Tits, are rarer birds with more restricted ranges, but where they do occur they all

regularly visit gardens and come to bird feeders.

Another well-represented garden group is the finches. Chaffinch, Greenfinch, Goldfinch and Siskin are all widespread and common, and readily use feeders and bird tables. Bullfinches and Lesser Redpolls are less common but still show up in many a rural garden.

The Robin is a classic garden bird, endearing itself to the gardener by perching on spade handles, nesting in watering cans and posing attractively on snowy foliage. Less obvious but equally common is the Dunnock, which hunts for insects, and plays out its famously complex sex life, in secluded spots in the undergrowth. A third small insectivore, the Wren, is also discreet and skulking but gives itself away with its lung busting, machine-gun rattle of a song.

If you have any area of lawn, the chances are you see

**Song Thrush in ivy berries**

Allowing ivy to grow on walls will provide cover for potential nesting birds, and eventually food, in the form of berries that will be popular with many species such as this Song Thrush.
*Nikon D2X, Sigma 300-800mm lens (at 650mm), ISO 200, 1/1000th sec at f8*

Blackbirds bouncing across it several times a day. These thrushes are also one of the likeliest candidates to be discovered nesting in a garden bush or hedge. Song Thrushes and Mistle Thrushes are also common garden birds, and winter may bring their northern relatives, Redwings and Fieldfares, to feed on windfall apples.

Several bird species like to nest on or in buildings. Starlings and House Sparrows are among them – both are in worryingly steep population decline at the

**White-crowned Sparrow**
What on earth is that? This strange bird that showed up in a Norfolk garden in early 2008 was a White-crowned Sparrow from North America – only the fourth ever to be found in Britain.
*Nikon D2X, Sigma 300-800mm lens (at 750mm), ISO 250, 1/200th sec at f5.6*

# Garden 'megas'

If you are a birdwatcher first and photographer second, you probably dream of finding a real rarity in your garden. If it ever happens, you'll definitely want to record the event on camera – although you may find yourself doing so alongside a couple of hundred other birdwatchers.

Some of the most famous long-staying mega-rarities to have visited Britain recently have based themselves in gardens. In Cley, Norfolk, a White-crowned Sparrow from North America stayed in a garden from late winter to spring 2008, gobbling up birdseed alongside Chaffinches and Greenfinches every day. In winter 2004, a dazzling Baltimore Oriole, also from North America, made an extended stay in a group of Oxford gardens, and was much photographed eating seed and oranges from bird tables.

moment, so do your best to encourage them if you have them nesting in your house or garden. The same goes for Common Swifts – you can't do much to persuade these insect hawkers to feed in your garden, but in this age of frantic home improvements, where nesting crannies are hard to find, providing a swift nestbox could really help out this spectacular summer visitor. House Martins glue their own mud nests to walls just under the eaves, but will use suitably placed special nestboxes too.

If you have mature trees in or around your garden you are likely to have visits from the striking Great Spotted Woodpecker and the athletic, aggressive Nuthatch. Both will use feeders and cause consternation among the smaller birds when they arrive.

Some larger birds that regularly use gardens include Woodpigeons, Collared Doves, Magpies, Jays, Jackdaws and Carrion Crows. All of them can be encouraged to visit, and linger, by provision of the right kinds of food. If you have a local population of Feral Pigeons, they will probably discover your bird table whether you want them to or not – but look out too for the similar but daintier Stock Dove.

If your garden attracts plenty of little birds, don't be surprised (and try not to be upset) if it also attracts a bigger bird that feeds on little birds. Sparrowhawks are the likeliest raptors to show up in the average garden, and can provide many a spectacular moment. The predator night shift may be filled by Tawny Owls, which are surprisingly common even in quite built-up areas providing there are some tall trees around.

Depending on its immediate surroundings, your garden's bird list may be boosted by farmland birds like Yellowhammers and Grey Partridges, birds of freshwater habitats like Kingfishers and Mallards, or woodland dwellers like Goldcrests and Spotted Flycatchers. Gardens at or near the coast may have regular visitations by seabirds, with Herring Gulls perhaps most likely, and they also have the potential for attracting something really unusual, perhaps a lost migrant from overseas. Whatever your interest in birds, you'll find that as soon as you start trying to photograph them, every one of them offers a tantalizing challenge.

**Tawny Owl**
Ivy-covered trees in larger gardens provide ideal daytime roost sites for Tawny Owls.
*Nikon D2X, Sigma 300-800mm lens (at 750mm), ISO 200, 1/80th sec at f5.6*

## Reptiles and amphibians

The UK has a relatively small number of native reptiles and amphibians, although we do also have quite a few 'introduced exotics' setting up home in odd corners of the nation. These animals are very inconspicuous most of the time, so a little detective work may be necessary to discover whether they are visiting your garden. They hibernate in winter.

The Slow-worm is the reptile most likely to be found in the average UK garden. These handsome creatures, which look like mini snakes but are actually legless lizards, are largely crepuscular and often spend the daytime in warm, humid hiding places such as under log piles or in compost heaps. You're most likely to chance upon a Slow-worm while doing garden chores, but it is worth having a (careful) search for them in suitable spots in spring and summer, and if you find any make sure that you leave some undisturbed corners for them to use as hibernating places in winter.

The Common or Viviparous Lizard is widespread and common in places, and may be found in larger, more rural gardens. It enjoys basking in the sun, so if you have this species in your garden it is a good idea to provide some flat, slightly elevated surfaces for them to sunbathe on – decking is a big favourite. Although they can move very fast, it's often possible to approach them

**Common Lizard**
Like other reptiles, Common Lizards run on heat. You're most likely to see them basking on warm surfaces (wooden decking is ideal) on hot days.
*Panasonic DMC-FZ18, ISO 100, 1/320th sec at f5.6*

closely if you move slowly and are careful.

Of the UK's three native snakes, Adders and Grass Snakes are the most common, but you'd be quite lucky to find either in your garden. Adders like warm, dry, often fairly open surroundings, while Grass Snakes are keen swimmers and most likely to be found near water.

There are lots of good reasons to have a garden pond – Common Toads and Common Frogs are two of them. These amphibians both need water to breed, they lay their eggs (spawn) in water and the young frogs and toads can't leave the water until they are mature. Adult Common Frogs, and especially adult Common Toads, are not so reliant on water in their day-to-day lives, and you may find them searching for insects and other creepy-crawlies to eat, or dozing in any damp, sheltered spot.

The most aquatic of the amphibians are the newts. There are three species in the UK, and any of them could show up in a garden pond, especially if yours is not too far from other bodies of water. The Smooth Newt is the most common.

## Fish

Unless you have a river or stream running through your garden, the chances are that the only fish you're likely to see are the ones living in your pond. If your pond is new you may well have put the fish in it yourself.

If you are making a new pond, or want to add some native fish to an existing pond, it is possible to buy (or catch from the wild) small species like Three-spined or Ten-spined Sticklebacks, or Minnows. Be warned though, that they feed on other aquatic animals, so your pond may not have as diverse a wildlife population as it would if it was fish-free. A garden pond is a small, enclosed environment and so is less likely to achieve a natural 'balance' than a bigger body of water that's connected to others through streams and rivers. In particular, newts and sticklebacks don't get on very well at all.

## Invertebrates

In terms of both numbers and variety, the invertebrates will outweigh their backboned equivalents by a huge margin in any garden. The majority of these little creeping, flying or swimming creatures are extremely small, extremely well hidden or both, and with the best will in the world you may never see them, let alone catch them on camera. However, there are still many more that have much more visual presence.

The larger flying insects are the most obvious and, to many, the most appealing invertebrate garden visitors. Showy butterflies, like the Red Admiral, Small Tortoiseshell and Peacock, are easily attracted to almost any garden. Less welcome, but equally common, are the Large and Small Whites, a.k.a. 'cabbage whites'. All of these species are nomadic by nature, roaming far and wide in search of food and breeding partners. Most other butterflies are less adventurous and you're only likely to see them in your garden if it, or its surroundings, have good supplies of the plant, or plant species, on which they lay their eggs. Many, like the Meadow Brown, Gatekeeper, Speckled Wood, and Small and Large Skippers, lay their eggs on native grasses. Most of the blues need downland or heathland flowers; an exception is the Holly Blue, which lays its eggs on holly or ivy (depending on the time of year). It is the blue most likely to be seen in gardens.

For every butterfly species in the UK, there are about 40 kinds of moths – so more than 2,000 in all. Most are nocturnal, but the canny wildlife photographer can find them at their daytime roosting places. Moths are also famously drawn to light – moth-traps use ultraviolet light to attract them, and an inventively designed box to

**Red Admiral**
Buddleia bushes are a magnet for wandering butterflies; plant one in your garden and it should attract species such as this Red Admiral, plus the Small Tortoiseshell, Comma and Peacock, almost anywhere in the UK.
*Nikon D2X, Nikkor 800mm lens, ISO 200, 1/400th sec at f11*

**Garden Tiger**

Although most moths are active at night some, such as the Silver Y and this Garden Tiger, are on the wing during the day, and are common visitors to some gardens.

*Nikon D1X, Nikkor 105mm macro lens, ISO 200, 1/80th sec at f11*

keep them prisoner until it's time to photograph them and release them the next day. These traps can be used to great effect in even very small spaces (see Chapter 6 for more on moth traps). Many moths are dozy and tractable in the daytime, and it's easy to 'arrange' them in the photographic set-up of your choice – just

## Indoor animals

Most of us want, not unreasonably, to keep the wildlife outside. Some wildlife wants to come inside, though, and not all of it is totally undesirable. Mice in your house are most likely to be House Mice, but in more rural parts of southern England they may be Yellow-necked Mice, which are attractive and not especially common little mammals that happen to like houses. You probably will want to evict them, and keep them out, but you might as well photograph them before you let them go. Use humane traps to catch them, and photograph them in a naturalistic set-up in a large

tank, before releasing them a long way from your house (or they'll move back in, unless you've found and blocked their access point or points).

If you have a shed or some other kind of outbuilding, you may find some wildlife moves in, especially if it is at all open to the elements. Various specie of spiders often set up home in sheltered places like this, while Small Tortoiseshell and Peacock butterflies like them for hibernating. In the countryside, sheds, barns and other open structures provide homes for nesting Swallows and sometimes Pied Wagtails. For a lucky few they may attract nesting Barn Owls.

remember to place them somewhere safe from predators if they don't want to fly away after the shoot. Some common and attractive moths you may find in your garden include Angle Shades, Magpie Moth, Silver Y, Garden Tiger, Swallow-tailed Moth and the various hawk-moths.

A flower-filled garden will attract all kinds of nectar-feeding insects. Bees are popular visitors, and with them come their stingless imitators, the hoverflies. Some beetles feed on nectar, while others patrol the ground, eating decaying plant or animal matter or chasing down less swiftly moving invertebrates. Everyone's favourite beetles, the ladybirds, are voracious hunters of smaller insects, especially aphids, while some species of ant enjoy a less one-sided relationship with aphids, 'milking' them for the honeydew they secrete.

A healthy wildlife pond is a great breeding ground for invertebrates, many of which are flying insects that

**Common Blue Damselflies mating**

A garden pond increases your chances of taking images like this of Common Blue Damselflies in their pre-mating 'tandem' pose. *Nikon D2X, Nikkor 800mm lens, ISO 200, 1/500th sec at f13*

spend their early lives foraging the pond floor. Make sure that your pond has plenty of plant stems at the edges to enable these creatures to climb out of the water and emerge from their wingless larval casings to begin their new lives – a great moment to record if you're lucky enough to witness it. Most spectacular are the dragonflies and their daintier cousins, the damselflies. Many 'dragons' travel considerable distances on their hunting forays, and you may see the larger species, such as Common and Southern Hawkers, over your garden even if there is no water nearby. 'Damsels' are also hunters of other insects, but they are

less powerful fliers, and often stick fairly close to their pond or river of origin. Large Red, Common Blue and Blue-tailed Damselflies are all common species.

Other flying insects that begin their lives underwater include caddis-flies, mayflies and stoneflies, as well as less appealing creatures such as midges and mosquitoes. Your pond may also attract more strictly aquatic insects like pond skaters and water-boatmen, both of which get about using the surface tension of the water to impressive (and photogenic) effect.

Slugs and snails aren't always popular with gardeners, but can make interesting photographic subjects. The banded snails (*Cepaea* species), such as White-lipped and Brown-lipped Snails, are especially attractive, and can provide an easily handled living element to set-up still-life photographs. Other garden invertebrates, such as centipedes, are fleeter of foot and more challenging to the photographer. Many species of spider are shy and hard to observe, but others play out intimate life-cycle episodes on full view.

Getting to know your garden 'mini-beasts' is a different kind of challenge to observing the larger and more familiar animals. However, the small stuff is the backbone of your garden ecosystem so, even if you don't really want to get up close and personal with creepy-crawlies, making your garden a hospitable place for them will make it a more appealing place for the more glamorous wildlife too.

**Large Red Damselfly**
Damselflies like this Large Red may breed in ponds in gardens, and are usually easier to photograph than the larger dragonflies, staying still for longer and allowing a closer approach.
*Nikon D300, Nikkor 105mm Macro lens, ISO 200, 1/320th sec at f11*

## Plants, fungi and other static elements

For many wildlife photographers, plants only exist to provide an attractive backdrop for the main focus of interest – the animal. However, you might find yourself drawn to photograph a plant for its own merits – it's hard to resist a perfect orchid or the variegated bark of a plane tree. Even if plants don't stir your photographic spirit it's important to pay attention to the ones in your garden – they play a huge part in determining what wildlife will be present, and they will often form a key element of your animal photographs. In Chapter 3 we look at choosing garden plants from a wildlife-friendly point of view.

Native plants, including some of the most photogenic, will be described as 'weeds' by many a narrow-minded gardener. Don't listen to them – beautiful flowering plants like Rosebay Willowherb, Bugle, Foxglove, Borage, Cuckoo-flower, speedwells, buttercups and even the humble Dandelion and Daisy are all worthy of your photographic attention.

Moreover, for native wildlife, native plants are best. Some exotic plants may produce explosions of flowers or bushels of berries, which attract wandering insects and birds respectively, but it is the native plants which will encourage wildlife to stick around and ecosystems to develop and grow. The humble Stinging Nettle, for example, famously supports 30 or 40 species of insect, all laying their eggs on this plant and no other. Native trees are even more important to all kinds of wildlife, so if you have any in your garden do your best to take care of them, and if you want to plant new trees, choose species that naturally belong in your part of the world.

Plants provide wildlife with shelter as well as food. Many garden birds nest in thick, scrubby bushes – a wall of thorns is an effective predator deterrent, so cultivating Blackberry thickets benefits them, as well as giving you a supply of tasty fruit. Ivy-clad walls provide homes for House Sparrows, so resist the temptation to rip the ivy down unless you absolutely have to. Decaying plant material may not look great, but it provides yet another wildlife habitat – your compost heap is probably teeming with invertebrates, and your log pile may shelter beetles, moths, toads and Hedgehogs.

Most of us only acknowledge fungi when crops of mushrooms appear on our lawns, but these represent only a small and (usually) transient component of our

gardens' fungal population. Out of sight, the soil and decaying leaf litter is packed with fine threads of fungal mycelia, absorbing nutrients, growing and spreading. Mushrooms and toadstools are the 'fruiting bodies' of the fungus, releasing reproductive spores.

Mushrooms and toadstools make attractive photographic subjects. Their appearance in gardens is hard to predict, but most appear in autumn. They may pop up overnight, especially after rain, but smaller kinds tend to dry up or disintegrate quickly, and most are eagerly devoured by snails and other animals, so if you see one you'd like to photograph, don't hang around.

Most animals leave signs of some kind indicating their presence. Not all of these signs may be the kinds of things you want to photograph – but others make interesting and appealing subjects, and have the added advantage of being portable, so you can use them to set up still-life arrangements, as well as to practise getting to grips with your camera's various settings. Snail shells, birds' feathers, discarded eggshells, gnawed nutshells, insect larval cases and the like can make fascinating photographs, either on their own or combined with other elements, like pebbles, twigs, fallen leaves and so on, to make naturalistic or outlandish set-ups. You can also use natural bits and pieces to enhance backdrops for planned photos of living, moving creatures.

### White Foxglove (*below left*)
Foxgloves are one of Britain's few biennials (plants which live for two years, flowering in their second year). Therefore you tend to get a good Foxglove year followed by one that is not as good. Look out for the less common white and pale pink forms among the usual cerise ones.
*Panasonic DMC-FZ18, ISO 100, 1/400th sec at f2.8*

### Scarlet Pimpernel (*below centre*)
A great name for a delightful little flower – Scarlet Pimpernel flowers close up by mid-afternoon, and also if the weather takes a turn for the worse, so it is best to choose a sunny morning to photograph them.
*Panasonic DMC-FZ18, ISO 100, 1/500th sec at f7.1*

### Blackberry flower (*below*)
Blackberry is one of the best plants you can have in your garden. The flowers produce abundant nectar before turning into tasty fruit, and the plant forms thorny thickets that make perfect nest sites for birds.
*Panasonic DMC-FZ18, ISO 100, 1/200th sec at f4*

# CHAPTER 2 Welcoming the wildlife

**Rose-coloured Starling**

Putting out food in your garden is a guaranteed way of attracting birds to feed; among the commoner species there is always the chance of an exotic-looking rarity such as this Rose-coloured Starling, which fed with Common Starlings on fat balls in a Lancashire garden for a few days in June 2008. *Nikon D300, Sigma 300-800mm lens (at 600mm), ISO 200, 1/250th sec at f5.6*

Supermodel Linda Evangelista famously stated that 'we don't wake up for less than $10,000 a day'. Hopefully, making your garden attractive to suitably photogenic wildlife won't require such a generous budget, but there are virtually no limits on the tricks you can use to boost its pulling power. This is not a comprehensive guide to wildlife gardening (many excellent books exist on the subject), but should give you some ideas and starting points, depending on whether you have access to a windowsill or a wilderness.

# No garden

Plenty of homes have no garden at all, and many such homes are in built-up areas with not that much wildlife around. If this is your situation, whether temporary or permanent, you'll need to be extra creative to bring wildlife into photographic range.

It's often said that in British cities you're never more than five metres away from a rat. I'm not sure of the truth of this, but would be most interested to see the corresponding statistic for Blue and Great Tits. These little birds are as adaptable and enterprising as any city high-flier, and they are among the birds you're most likely to be able to attract to a special window bird feeder in even the most urban setting. These clever contraptions stick to window glass with rubber suckers strong enough to bear the weight of the full feeder plus a few small, feathery visitors, and they come in tray or tube form. Shelled sunflower seeds are probably the best bait – scatter a few on the windowsill if you have one, to help get the birds' attention. In the right environment, your window feeder may also attract finches and sparrows.

The trouble with these feeders is that they are difficult to disguise, so it is hard to get natural-looking shots. You might want to experiment with fixing some foliage near, or around, the feeder. Another issue is that you will always be shooting through glass – there isn't much you can do about this except make sure the windows are clean, and don't use flash as it will just bounce off the glass and give you a black photo with a bright spot of glare.

In the breeding season, you may have some luck attracting birds if you put out nesting material.

**Sparrow terrace**
Nestboxes like this 'terrace' for three House Sparrow families can be fixed to a wall just as easily as a tree, and nearby tree branches provide perfect perches for the birds as they go to and fro.

Anything fibrous and/or soft could work: straw, hair (human or animal), feathers or pieces of wool are all worth trying. Tie the material up in a bundle, so the birds have to spend a moment pulling loose the pieces they want, and fix to the wall or window, somewhere where there's a flat surface that the birds can perch on.

If you are able to fix things to the wall of your home, within sight of a window, you could try a nestbox. Your best bet is a shop-bought or home-made, small, wooden nestbox, about 25 x 15 x 15cm, with a 25-28mm circular entrance hole at least 12.5cm above the floor of the box. This design will work for Blue and Great Tits. You can also build, or buy, boxes designed for Starlings and House Sparrows, as well as imitation mud nests to go under the eaves and hopefully attract House Martins.

Insects may use boxes too. Enterprising manufacturers have designed boxes to attract hibernating lacewings, ladybirds and bees – if you want to make your own, try fixing open-ended lengths of bamboo, or other hollow tubes, inside a wooden box frame (it's important that all the wood you use is untreated).

If you leave your curtains open and lights on in the summer, you're likely to attract moths now and then, especially if you are near to some green spaces. Check the walls around the window the next day – some of your visitors may stick around. For a more focused approach, you could operate a modest moth trap (see Chapter 6), if you have a sufficiently broad and secure windowsill.

Windowsills open up the possibility of window boxes – a great way to bring flying insects into view. Choose a diverse range of plants with plenty of native species, including some good nectar flowers – herbs like thyme and marjoram are good choices for wildlife as well as cookery. Night-fragranced flowers, like Honeysuckle and Red Campion, will appeal to moths.

Finally, remember you can still enjoy 'proper' garden wildlife photography without having a garden of your own – just use someone else's, or visit your local public garden.

**Large Emerald**

If last night was warm and you had your lights on until late, take a look on and around the window frame in the morning to see if any moths have stayed over. The handsome Large Emerald is one of many species that are attracted to light.

# Flat out

If you live in a flat on the first floor or above, you may have a share in a communal garden – either just an agreement for shared use of the whole space, or your own dedicated patch of garden. Either way, it will pay to get friendly with your neighbours and convince them to let you maintain some, or all, of the garden as a wildlife-friendly space – offering to do more than your share of the maintenance could work wonders!

With no garden at all, hopefully you will have a good view to make up for it. Depending on where you live, you may have regular flypasts of birds, including 'non-garden species', providing opportunities to practise your panning and zooming skills.

# The stone garden

Is your garden essentially a piece of pavement surrounded by a fence? While not an obvious choice for the wildlife enthusiast, the patio garden has its advantages, particularly for those who, for whatever reason, don't wish to get involved in the often hard work of maintaining a conventional garden. Even if you don't like your patio garden, you may not have the time, energy, or (in the case of rented homes) permission to dig up the stones and start again. Don't despair – there is much you can do in a garden of this type to bring in more wildlife.

You probably already have some plants in containers. To bring in more wildlife, get adventurous and add some more sizeable planters stocked with native plant communities. Experiment with combinations – you could try one with mixed grasses and meadow flowers, or berry-bearing shrubs. The flowers of teasels and thistles attract insects, while their seeds appeal strongly to Goldfinches. Some non-native plants are also worth including, such as buddleias for their nectar and cotoneasters for their abundant red berries. Make sure your pots contain some early- and late-flowering

### Container pond
Water, even in tiny quantities, is an essential in any garden. A small container pond like this provides drinking water for animals and will support a small but diversity-enhancing ecosystem of its own.

**Honeysuckle**

If your garden is bounded by fences or walls, cultivate flowering climbers like Honeysuckle on them to disguise their contours and to provide food and shelter for wildlife.
*Panasonic DMC-FZ18, ISO 100, 1/250th sec at f4*

plants for those insects that are on the wing at the end of the season – many bulbs are good spring options, while Ivy is an excellent late autumn choice.

Containers (as long as they're watertight) can also be used to make ponds. At the simplest level, you can make (from any shallow container) or buy a birdbath and keep it topped up with tap water, if the rain doesn't do the job. This will attract birds to drink and bathe, and perhaps mammals will come and drink too.

A larger container could accommodate something approaching a natural pond. Use stones in the bottom to create a level slope right up to the edges – steep sides are dangerous for small mammals and unhelpful to emerging insects. Adding aquatic plants (again, native species are best) will increase your pond's appeal to insects, which in turn attract birds as well as frogs, toads and newts. Make sure the container pond is placed somewhere where non-flying visitors can get at it.

For bird-feeding stations, the sky's the limit – a good start would be a bird table mounted on a post, with hooks attached for hanging feeders. Try leaving food out for mammals too, especially if you know they are already visiting. Dog food works well for Hedgehogs and foxes, while mice, voles and squirrels will enjoy

nuts and seeds. Just be mindful that baiting like this may also attract less desirable elements – if you need to discourage rats you'll have to forget the ground baiting and also be disciplined about cleaning up bird-table spillages. Mice and squirrels are quite able to access most bird tables anyway.

When planning your container garden, think about the kinds of photos you want to take, especially of the larger animals where you'll inevitably have less control over the amount of backdrop the images will include. Providing naturalistic perching options near your bird table, or placing logs on the ground by the container pond, will help create the impression of a wilder setting if that's what you want to achieve, but not if there's a picket fence right in the way. Consider disguising sections of wall or fence with climbing foliage – honeysuckle and jasmine are ideal for the job, and will attract plenty of insects and provide nest sites for birds into the bargain.

# The typical garden

Gardens in the UK vary tremendously in size, shape, soil composition, surrounding environment and so on. Let's picture an average suburban garden, somewhere between 50 and 150 square metres in size, one in a row of similar gardens, each with a section or two of lawn, one or two modest-sized trees, a paved or decked area for sitting out, perhaps a pond and some flowerbeds. There is probably a patch of woodland or parkland within a couple of miles, with a lake, river or stream. Hopefully this fictitious garden has at least some elements in common with your own.

**A medium-sized garden**

An average UK garden, with lawn, flowerbeds and a couple of trees. There's room for a bird-feeding station and somewhere to dry the clothes too, and lots of nooks and crannies for wildlife (and photographers) to hide in.

**The lawn**

A neatly trimmed lawn may look nice but it's not a particularly inviting habitat for wildlife. One of the best, and easiest, things you can do to encourage wildlife, especially insects, is to leave a patch of your lawn (or all of it if you like) un-mown through the summer, cutting it only in late July or August. This is a great start for encouraging a more diverse grassland plant community. If you want to take the next step towards cultivating your own mini-meadow, you could clear an area of lawn completely, and then sow the soil with a mixture of fine grasses and wild flower seeds. The exact mix that works best will depend on your soil type and how sunny your

garden is. The wild flowers will attract insects, and their seeds will provide a great natural food source for birds.

### Flowerbeds

The exposed soil in flowerbeds makes for easy foraging for thrushes, Robins and other insect-eating birds. By night, their place may be taken by Hedgehogs and other small mammals, if you're lucky. In addition to your favourite conventional garden flowers, make room in your beds for some attractive native species – Bluebells, campions, Wood Anemones, dead-nettles, Bugle and Wild Thyme for example – all of these will support more diverse insect communities than the non-natives. Patches of exposed mud can also supply vital nesting materials for birds.

### Trees

As a general rule, deciduous trees are better for wildlife than conifers, and (as usual)

**Gatekeeper**
The Gatekeeper is not a common visitor to most gardens, but those with a wild area of long grass and brambles will stand a good chance of attracting one, especially in southern England.
*Nikon D1X, Nikkor 105mm macro lens,*
*ISO 200, 1/200th sec at f8*

native species beat exotics. Even a single, modest-sized tree is a boon for any garden, especially if there are trees in other gardens as well, because then, as far as the wildlife is concerned, your tree becomes part of a woodland, with every inch of it a potential home for living things. If space allows, consider planting more trees – they extend the effective reach of your garden upwards as well as outwards and provide instant photographic sets for your animal subjects to pose in. The more adventurous among you might even consider building a tree-house to use as a permanent photography hide, providing a new perspective onto your garden and its wildlife.

Vantage points
**Vantage points** If you have, or are planning to add, an area of patio, decking or gravel for a bit of garden furniture, this might not in itself provide good wildlife habitat, but it does provide potentially good photographer habitat. The more time you spend sitting out in your garden, the more accustomed your birds will become to your presence. Such spaces could also prove comfortable and convenient locations for placing photography hides.

### Woodpile

Ah, rotting wood – lunch for beetle grubs and a host of other invertebrates, and shelter for amphibians. Make sure your garden includes a nice, soggy woodpile or two.

**Water** If your garden doesn't already have a pond, consider adding one – the benefit to wildlife, and wildlife photographers, cannot be overstated. When planning a pond, think about the animals you want to attract and the photos you want to take. Ideally your pond will have some fairly deep water in parts, but a gradually sloping bank so animals can drink from it easily and safely. Make sure you'll have a clear view of the pond from a spot where you'll be able to watch quietly without disturbing the visitors, and choose a site with good light (sunny ponds are better for wildlife too) and an appealing backdrop. When landscaping the pond itself, consider aesthetics as well as animal appeal – you may want to give your pond a natural appearance by disguising its man-made elements; using plenty of appealing aquatic plants will help with this. Include some attractive shrubs to provide photogenic resting places for birds waiting to drink or drying off after a bath. Adding goldfish won't do your pond wildlife any favours, although a few small native fish (see Chapter 2) won't do much harm in a larger pond. Clear excess vegetation from your pond in autumn, but leave it by the pond's side for a day or two before composting it, so that any small animals caught up in it can return to the water. If you have a pond, make sure you have an undisturbed woodpile too, as this will provide shelter for any amphibians that visit the pond, and will encourage them to make a permanent home in your garden.

### Shrubs and hedges

Whether your garden is bounded by walls or fences, you can add another wildlife boost, and disguise these non-natural features at the same time, using bushes and climbers. Some brick walls are quite photogenic, and some fences can't cope with the weight of an impromptu hedge leaning against them, but if you can cultivate some species of native shrubs, you'll provide your wildlife with another natural food source in the form of nectar and, later, berries, as well as a safe and sheltered place to live and breed. Prickly bushes like Blackberry, Blackthorn and Hawthorn are best – nesting birds will be extra safe from predators inside a dense, thorny thicket. Blackberry flowers are very attractive to nectar-feeding insects. Another nectar bearer to consider is buddleia – non-native, but despite this it's well worth including a bush or two in a wildlife garden as they really are butterfly magnets.

**Redwing with berry**
Berry-bearing shrubs planted in the garden can lead to many species of birds visiting to feed; an image of a bird in a berry-covered tree, or shrub, makes for a very attractive photograph. Fieldfares, Mistle and Song Thrushes, Blackbirds and Redwings, as in this shot, may all visit during the winter.
*Nikon D2X, Sigma 300-800mm lens (at 750mm), ISO 200, 1/500th sec at f5.6*

### Compost heaps

Lots of tiny invertebrates depend on decaying plant and animal matter. By allowing garden and kitchen waste to rot away in an open compost heap, you provide yet another productive wildlife habitat, as well as a source of free, top-quality soil.

Feeding the birds Having sorted out the basics of your garden ecosystem, you can now turn your attention to the added extras. Some kind of bird-feeding station is a must. Always position your bird tables and feeders close to some form of cover. This will help the birds to escape during a sudden Sparrowhawk or cat attack, and to feel more confident about using the table. It will also provide you with more photographic options than just 'bird sitting on feeder/table', as they will use nearby natural perches as launch pads.

Feeders come in all shapes and sizes, and there's an equally bewildering array of bird foods on the market. Your best bet is to offer a selection. Shelled sunflower seeds are popular with many tits and finches – offer them in tube feeders for a longer lifespan than if they're out on the bird table. Nyjer seed is popular with Goldfinches – special tube feeders with small holes are available for dispensing these tiny, fine seeds. Peanuts go down well with tits, Siskins, Nuthatches and Great Spotted Woodpeckers, but don't offer whole peanuts in the breeding season as chicks may choke on them – wire mesh feeders are good for peanuts as the birds can only extract them in fragments.

'Bird cake' – a mixture of seeds, and sometimes dried insects, mixed up with fat to form solid blocks – is a nutritious food that you can buy or make yourself – wire 'cage' feeders are best for dispensing it. If you really want your garden birds to love you, offer live food – mealworms or waxworms – in dedicated feeders.

Bird tables set high above the ground are safe from cats, but some birds are dedicated ground feeders and will prefer a table at or just above ground level. Be aware, however, that food left on the ground for birds may attract rats. You can offer all manner of foods on bird tables – kitchen scraps and leftovers are often acceptable, mixed seed can be scattered in handfuls

# The ethics of bird feeding

On the face of it, feeding wild birds is a straightforward 'good thing to do', whether you want to photograph them or not. However, you may have, or you might develop, qualms about it for a variety of reasons.

**'It's unnatural. We shouldn't make the birds dependent on artificial food sources.'**
Undoubtedly feeding the birds is unnatural; however, so is the extent to which we've modified our landscape – the garden itself is an unnatural environment. Most of our garden birds evolved as woodland birds, and the UK has lost 45 per cent of its woodland in the last 60 years alone, with an inevitable impact on bird populations. Feeding them could be seen as a way to redress the balance. It is a commitment; if you feed birds for a while and then stop, the birds may suffer. However, studies have shown that garden birds range quite widely in the winter, so the five Blue Tits you see on your feeder at various points through the day are not likely to be the same birds every time, but part of a much larger population that tours lots of different gardens in your area.

**'A Sparrowhawk is killing my garden birds. My feeding station is nothing but a Sparrowhawk McDonalds, and soon the little birds will all be gone.'** Seeing your garden birds killed by Sparrowhawks can be upsetting, and you may feel guilty for placing the birds in a dangerous situation, as well as mourn the loss of individual birds. However, Sparrowhawks and their prey have lived together for millennia – the hawk can only survive if there is a thriving population of prey species for it to feed on. The presence of a top predator is clear evidence that your garden ecosystem is flourishing. Meanwhile, if you site your feeding station close to suitable cover, you'll give the little birds a fighting chance of escape when the hawk comes.

**'There are cats in my garden. I am luring the garden birds to their doom.'** The domestic cat is a different case from the Sparrowhawk. Because cats are pets and get fed whether or not they eat wild

and windfall fruit is very popular with thrushes. A chunk of raw beef fat provides valuable calories in cold winters – mammals (including cats) will carry it off if they can reach it, but a piece nailed to a tree will last a surprisingly long time and is very likely to interest your local Great Spotted Woodpecker.

### Unwelcome visitor

It has to be said that Brown Rats are not very welcome in most people's gardens; to discourage them bird tables need to be kept clean and any spillage cleaned from the floor.

*Nikon D300, Sigma 300-800mm lens (at 750mm), ISO 400, 1/100th sec at f5.6*

birds, their presence and survival doesn't depend on there being healthy numbers of their prey species. The best thing is to try to keep cats out of your garden. If you have a cat, keep it indoors if you can. As long as it has enough indoor space and gets enough exercise and attention, the average cat will be fine as a house cat. If that's not possible, keep it in overnight, as most hunting takes place at night, and at dusk and dawn, and fit a couple of bells to its collar (a slowly stalking cat won't jiggle a single bell, but two bells will bump together). If your problem is your neighbours' cats, there are various methods at your disposal. First of all you can try to 'cat proof' the boundaries of your garden – high fences and/or dense hedges will help, though remember cats are adept tree climbers. You can also buy chemical or sonic repellents. Lion dung (available from some gardening retailers) scattered in flowerbeds apparently works well, convincing the cat that your garden is home to a much bigger and scarier predator. Some plants, such as *Coleus canina*, apparently deter cats. And finally, lying in wait with a super-soaker water pistol is a popular strategy. A dousing with cold water won't hurt the cat but may permanently put it off coming into your garden.

### Domestic cat

Here comes trouble… love them or hate them, cats don't mix well with wildlife photography. Do your best to discourage them if you don't want your subjects to be scared away or eaten.

*Nikon D2X, Sigma 300-800mm lens (at 390mm), ISO 400, 1/50th sec at f5.6*

### Beyond bird-feeders

Squirrels (both species) will use bird tables and feeders, as will mice – sometimes. A feeding table especially for small rodents is best placed in a sheltered position in the midst of easily climbable twigs and branches – make sure there is a clear line of sight for you and your camera though. Bait it with whole nuts and sweet titbits like dried fruit.

Many animals will seek out some kind of sheltered cavity for breeding or hibernating, and man-made substitutes are often more than acceptable. Some examples are discussed above under 'No Garden'. The bigger your garden, the more you can go to town with animal nestboxes and shelters. They can vary from the elaborate, to the very simple: 'sparrow terraces' offer a stylish communal living solution for multiple pairs of House Sparrows, while a half-buried, half-broken stone flowerpot could provide a dream home for a toad. You can buy, or make, roosting boxes for bats, shelters for Hedgehogs, homes for bumblebees and specially designed nestboxes for all manner of birds from Common Swifts and Swallows, to Tawny Owls and Kestrels. Place nestboxes carefully, choosing positions that will be safe for both the adults and the baby birds when they emerge. Many nestboxes and shelters won't provide great photo opportunities in themselves, but the wildlife they attract will hopefully make use of the more photogenic parts of your garden too.

**Red Squirrel on nut feeder**
Unlike the Grey, the Red Squirrel is a natural inhabitant of Britain, so if you are lucky enough to have it visiting your garden, make it very welcome. As this image shows, Reds do enjoy peanuts, and can be attracted down, if they are in the area, by this food. It is then just a matter of waiting for them to sit or climb along tree branches for a more natural shot. Incidentally, the pelage of this Red Squirrel shows an interesting two-tone effect due to moult.
*Nikon D300, Sigma 300-800mm lens (at 550mm), ISO 250, 1/125th sec at f5.6*

# Large gardens

If you're lucky enough to have a rambling rural garden, you probably enjoy plenty of wildlife already. Much of what was written in the 'typical garden' section above will apply to you, only on a larger scale – for example, you could create multiple ponds and feeding stations. Here we concentrate on things you can do to attract animals more typical of the wider countryside into your own private nature reserve.

**Dry stones**
Building a dry-stone wall is harder than it looks – as there's nothing sticking the stones to each other you need to fit them together with great care. The labyrinth of tunnels between the stones acts as a great habitat for small mammals, including Stoats and Weasels.

## Hedges and dry-stone walls

Features like this are great for dividing up your garden. Predators like Stoats, Weasels and Sparrowhawks like to follow linear features like these when they hunt, and both hedges and dry-stone walls provide a multitude of hiding holes for animals. The ideal wildlife hedge is dense from root to tip, contains a good variety of shrub species and has flowery, grassy banks. It will attract nesting birds like warblers and finches, provide a wealth of insect and plant food for shrews, mice and voles, and offer a profusion of flowers for summer insects and berries for birds in autumn and winter. Prune a new hedge aggressively at first to encourage dense lower level growth, but be sparing when cutting back established hedges (and leave them well alone in the nesting season). Your dry-stone wall should develop attractive moss and lichen communities and provide an appealing resting place (and photographic setting) for birds and insects.

## Water – the next level

As far as ponds are concerned, the bigger the better. A really decent-sized pond may attract swimming birds like Moorhens, and if you encourage marshy patches, or a reedbed, to develop you could attract a passing Reed Bunting, or Sedge or Reed Warbler.

Larger ponds can support a few native fish as well as a thriving insect community – if you do have fish in your pond it may be visited by Grey Herons, or even Kingfishers. If you have a stream running through your garden, it may be possible to form a stream-fed pond, which will develop a different – and probably richer – wildlife community than an isolated pond.

**Grey Heron**
Grey Herons visiting your garden may be bad news if you have a pond full of prize Koi Carp, but they are undeniably handsome birds and their slow, deliberate movements make them good photographic subjects.
*Panasonic DMC-FZ18, ISO 100, 1/400th sec at f5.6*

**Hide**
Retailers like Wildlife-watching Supplies sell a selection of purpose-designed hides, many of which are reasonably priced and easy for you to set up in your own garden.

**Fox**
Do not disturb. It might be your garden, but it is home for the animals that live there so don't hassle them unduly. This rather threadbare old Fox was having a sleep in the sunshine – better to settle for a less exciting photo than to wake him up.
*Panasonic DMC-FZ18, ISO 100, 1/250th sec at f4.2*

### Growing a woodland

Woodland management is not for the faint-hearted, but if you have the space and energy, adding a small copse of trees will send your garden's wildlife appeal skyrocketing in years to come. Select native trees (choose species which are thriving in your local area) and space them out so that a healthy understorey can develop. Allowing your garden to grade into woodland through an area of rough, scrubby grassland simulates natural conditions very effectively. You can incorporate trails and permanent hides that will allow you to get close to your woodland wildlife right from the start.

### Hide heaven

A large garden is a perfect playground for the amateur hide builder. Use your garden's natural corridors and barriers to provide cover, and experiment with a variety of hide types, from a simple screen to an adapted garden shed with all the comforts of home. You can buy pre-made simple, or complex, hides from specialist retailers too. Site your

hides so they overlook your garden's most attractive wildlife features – a pond or a feeding station are the obvious choices, and include hides at a variety of levels – a low-slung hide that enables you to photograph drinking birds at eye-level is an exciting option if you don't mind spending time flat on your belly, and tree hides can be great fun.

## Your own nature reserve?

If you really are blessed with outdoor space and are keen to make the very most of it, you should consider taking some kind of formal land-management training, to develop the practical skills you'll need to develop the habitats to their highest potential. The Royal Society for the Protection of Birds (RSPB) offers short courses in land management for conservation, as do various other conservation bodies. For more in-depth training you can study wildlife and land management at degree level at a number of universities.

# CHAPTER 3 Kitted out

## Using a compact
Don't give up if your funds won't run to an SLR camera with mega-telephoto lens – there is much you can achieve with a simple compact. Many compacts are very good at close-up photography.
*Panasonic DMC-FZ18, ISO 100, 1/160th sec at f2.8*

Whether your garden is already a wildlife paradise or at stage one of an ambitious overhaul, there's no reason to wait before launching yourself, camera-first, at whatever wildlife you can find. You may already own a camera you're happy with, but if you want to upgrade, or if you're poised to make your first camera purchase, it's worth taking some time to figure out exactly what you want. Of course, budget counts and a top-end SLR (single-lens reflex) camera with a selection of telephoto, wide-angle and macro lenses is going to enable you to take better photos of a wider range of subjects than a bargain compact. However, any camera can potentially take good shots if you hone your skills well and recognize its strengths and weaknesses.

**Photographers**
Photographers and their equipment; from a digiscope set-up to a tripod-mounted telephoto lens or a hand-held lens. All give decent results providing camera shake can be avoided.
*Nikon D2X, Sigma 300-800mm lens (at 300mm), ISO 200, 1/400th sec f8*

## Film or digital?

Most photographers have already made the switch from a film to a digital camera, and look back on the days of posting off a film for processing – perhaps weeks or months after its first shots were taken – with a sense of 'how did we put up with that' amusement. However, of those still using film cameras today, many are professionals. The digital medium certainly provides more freedom and flexibility, but does it still trail behind the original format in terms of quality?

There's no definitive answer. Digital technology has moved ahead so fast that for many its quality is indistinguishable from film, and most professionals made the switch years ago, but some still swear they never will. However, for any amateur, the advantages of digital have to outweigh any benefits of using film. You can take as many shots as you like for no extra cost, and experiment with different settings and see the results instantly – so you'll learn much more quickly. You can review them instantly, delete them if you don't like them, store them by the thousand on your computer, print them out to any size you want and experiment and improve upon them if they need it. You don't need a darkroom full of bubbling cauldrons to process the images yourself, just a computer with photo-editing software, and you can

**Migrant Hawker**
The most significant advantage that digital cameras have over film is probably the fact that many images can be taken without any extra cost involved. This shot of a flying Migrant Hawker dragonfly is not an easy image to take, but as you can practise all you like without any expense, there is nothing to lose by trying.
*Nikon D2X, Nikkor 300mm lens, ISO 200, 1/500th sec at f5.6*

tweak and modify every image to produce countless alternative versions of the same photo – all for no cost beyond powering the hardware itself. As arguments go, for most of us the film versus digital debate is as close to a 'no-brainer' as you would be likely to find anywhere.

# Phone cameras

The addition of a basic digital camera to a mobile phone used to be a nice gimmick.

Today, 'phone cams' have become very sophisticated, and phones with good cameras come with plenty of internal storage space (as well as the option to add memory cards), so you can take and store plenty of images alongside your music and video files – actually using one of these things to make a phone call is a bit like playing Solitaire on a NASA super-computer.

Even so, we wouldn't recommend having one of these as your primary camera – marvellous though they are they are still pretty limited, and the last thing

you want is for the phone to start ringing just as you're crouched in your hide, lining up a shot of your garden's first Badger.

# Compact or SLR?

The chief advantage of the compact is in the name – it's small, self-contained, you can take it anywhere. Most compacts are significantly cheaper than even entry-level SLRs too. The SLR scores over the compact for versatility – you can switch lenses to fill your frame with everything from tiny insects to distant birds in treetops. SLRs tend to have more sophisticated optics and sensors, and give you a greater range of options, and degree of control over the parameters that affect the way your photos turn out – shutter speed, aperture, ISO rating and so on. Somewhere in between are the so-called 'ultra-zoom' compacts, which offer much more telephoto power than standard compacts but are accordingly chunkier and pricier. Many compacts offer you the option to attach telephoto converters and macro filters, but optical quality will often suffer as a result.

## Parts of a camera

### LENS

This is the tube down which light travels into the camera and onto the sensor. Its sides are light-proofed, and it contains various glass elements to focus, and perhaps magnify, the image. In compact cameras the lens is fixed to the camera, in SLRs lenses are independent entities and can be swapped around as you wish. The first sheet of glass that the light hits is called the objective lens – in longer lenses particularly, the width of this lens makes a real difference to how well the lens works in low light, with bigger objectives performing better.

### LENS TYPES

Prime lenses have a single, fixed focal length, while zoom lenses have adjustable focal length – nearly all compacts have zoom lenses. The term 'digital zoom' just means you can set the camera to enlarge a part of the image – with a corresponding loss in quality – so digital zoom is no substitute for real optical zoom. The focal length of a lens is expressed in millimetres (for example, 35mm, 300mm) – the higher the number the more the lens magnifies its image. Very short lenses are called 'wide-angle' as they see a wider picture than the human eye, while long lenses are 'telephotos', and lenses that can focus on extremely close objects are 'macros'. In compact cameras, maximum focal length is often expressed as a ratio of the lens' shortest focal length – so a compact with a 35-105mm lens and another with a 50-150mm lens might both be described as '3x zoom', even though the former has a shorter maximum focal length than the latter. More sophisticated SLR lenses have features like image stabilization to control camera shake, and apochromatic adjustment to reduce chromatic aberration (colour 'fringing' around object edges).

### AUTOFOCUS AND MANUAL FOCUS SYSTEMS

Most digital cameras have reasonably sophisticated autofocus, which works by either focusing on the exact centre of the viewfinder, or on some other given point or points on the viewfinder, or by detecting areas of contrast (or some combination of these). Many cameras let you find your preferred point of focus, then reframe the image without losing that point. Impressive though it often is, autofocus is also perhaps the one automatic feature most likely to let you down, as the camera fails to fix onto what you want it to, or takes too long to do so. For this reason, until someone invents psychically activated autofocus it's a very good idea to thoroughly familiarize yourself with your camera's manual-focus mode too, if it has one.

## SHUTTER BUTTON

This is the button you press to take a photo. Usually, pressing the shutter button gently will activate auto-focusing and show you what your photo will look like (as well as displaying what the aperture and shutter speed settings will be), while a firmer press will open the shutter and take the photo.

## OTHER CONTROLS

There will probably be a settings wheel next to the shutter button, from which you'll choose between the camera's different exposure modes. Depending on the camera, there will be various buttons and levers to control things like flash, switching between manual and autofocus, setting macro modes and so on.

## APERTURE

This is the opening in the lens that determines how much light goes through to the camera's sensor to record an image. Like the pupil of an eye, the aperture can become wider to admit more light, or close up to restrict the amount of light getting in. This helps make sure that the photo is neither overexposed (too much light, giving a bleached-out image) nor underexposed (insufficient light, giving an image that's too dark). Apertures are expressed as 'f-numbers' – for example, f2.8, f22, and so on. Compacts will generally have a narrower aperture range than SLR lenses. The low end of the available aperture range is affected by physical factors – the larger its objective lens, the more light a lens can admit and thus the smaller its potential aperture. Aperture also controls depth of field (see page 52).

## SENSOR

Like the retina of your eye, or the film itself in a film camera, the sensor is the final destination of the light that enters a camera via its lens. The sensor converts the light into digital information, forming the photograph. The larger the sensor, the more detail it can potentially reveal.

## VIEW SCREEN

Good photographers, like gunslingers, always needed to master the ability to shoot 'from the hip' for when there wasn't time to lift the instrument to the eye. With the advent of the view screen, ordinary people can do it with ease too. The view screen and the viewfinder show you the same digital representation of the scene your camera is pointing at (you may be surprised to learn that the viewfinder image is not 'real' in most digital cameras), which is what the sensor will record when you press the shutter. You can use either of them to frame your photographs as well as review the images you've already taken. The view screen is great for showing off your photos to a crowd in the pub, but it really comes into its own when you're using a compact camera to take a macro shot of an insect on a plant – you can hold the camera close to your subject without having to poke your face into a mass of stinging nettles. Needless to say, bigger is better.

## BUILT-IN FLASH

If the light around isn't enough for aperture and shutter speed to give you a sharp and properly exposed image, your camera's automatic flash may be activated to give an extra burst of light when you take the photo. Most cameras have some form of automatic flash, although they vary widely in their sophistication and effectiveness. Nothing spoils an image more thoroughly than indiscriminate use of flash, so look out for a camera that gives you full control over how, and how much, flash is used.

*continued overleaf*

## Parts of a camera *continued*

**Starling 1**
A standard portrait shot of a moulting adult Starling, taken in June; at this size of reproduction, and at full frame, there is no sign of any noise or pixels.
*Nikon D300, Sigma 300-800mm lens (at 600mm), ISO 200, 1/250th sec at f5.6*

**Starling 2**
This is the same photo as the one on the left, but cropped to show just the bird's head and bill, and at this size the pixels that make up the digital image become very noticeable.

### MEGAPIXELS

A pixel is a single unit of information in a digital image. If you zoom right into a digital photo on your computer, what you see will eventually turn into a grid of squares, each square a single colour and tone. The more of these squares in an image, the more detailed the image can potentially be, as there's more room for smooth transitions from colour to colour. A megapixel is one million pixels. Therefore a seven megapixel camera records images that are made up of seven million pixels. The number of megapixels a camera can record works alongside the size of its sensor. Cramming vast amounts of pixels onto a tiny sensor is pointless as each pixel will be too small to record any meaningful light information.

### MEMORY AND FILE SIZES

Images on a digital camera are stored on memory cards. Your camera will have a small integral memory card, and a storage slot to take another, removable card. The file sizes your camera can manage are expressed by width in pixels x length in pixels. Larger files can contain more detail, and will look good printed out at larger sizes, but conversely they take up more space on your memory cards. You should be able to choose from a selection of image sizes – more advanced cameras will give you exact dimensions, while basic compacts may just give you the options of 'small, medium or large'.

### FILE TYPES

Most cameras produce images in the JPG (jpeg) file format by default. JPG is a compressed file format, so you can fit more of them on your memory card. If you change to shooting in RAW mode you will make uncompressed images with more potential detail, but you will need to recover that detail yourself using image-editing software on your computer.

# Simple compacts

A bewildering array of manufacturers offers compact cameras with a wide range of specifications and prices. You can pick one up for as little as £30, but it's perfectly possible to spend hundreds. For wildlife photography, one of the first factors to consider is optical zoom, and in the crudest sense, the more the better. However, there's no point filling the frame with your subject if the result is a poor-quality blurry, flat or 'noisy' (speckled) image. Take your time when choosing a camera – read impartial reviews, talk to other camera owners and take every chance you get to actually handle, and use, cameras in the right price range for you.

The number of megapixels determines, in broad terms, how much detail the camera can record. However, it works in tandem with the size of the camera's sensor. Beyond a certain point, extra megapixels make no perceptible difference to image quality if there isn't a corresponding increase in sensor size – the individual pixels are too tiny to register any worthwhile light and colour information.

Every compact camera should have a basic 'point and shoot' mode that will control aperture, shutter speed, autofocus and flash to produce acceptable images for even the most inexperienced camera-wielder. However, once you know what you're doing you're going to want to get experimental, and start taking control of these settings yourself. Compacts vary a great deal in terms of how much control they can give the user, and this is where you'll have to read the detailed specs and, even better, some impartial reviews. You'll probably want an aperture-priority mode, a shutter-speed priority mode, a range of ISO settings, adjustable levels of flash rather than 'all or nothing' and the option to use manual focus.

Other factors to consider include the size of the view screen (big is good), the way the autofocus system works (see 'Parts of a camera'), what kinds of accessories you can use with the camera, how easily you can fit a digiscoping adaptor if this kind of photography interests you (see page 50) and how well any special modes like macro work.

**Coolpix L5**
The Nikon Coolpix L5 is a high-spec, but lightweight, digital compact with a modest zoom lens and a clear, straightforward layout.

**Birdwatcher using compact camera held to telescope**
This is digiscoping in its simplest form: a birdwatcher holds a small compact camera to the eyepiece of his telescope and simply presses the shutter.

## Digiscoping

Digiscoping is the practice of fixing a compact digital camera to a telescope, so the latter works as a long telephoto lens. This style of photography is very popular with birdwatchers that tend to carry a telescope around with them anyway – it gives them a way to photograph distant birds without needing to carry a huge lens around as well. The camera is attached to the 'scope' by means of a special adaptor that holds everything steady and blocks outside light while channelling all the light passing through the scope into the camera. How good the resulting images are depends on the quality of all the

# Super-zoom compacts

These cameras, also known as 'bridge' cameras, or 'crossovers', look at first glance like SLRs. They are bulkier than compacts and have a contoured shape with a 'grip' rather than being flat, but they don't have interchangeable lenses. Instead, the one lens is designed to do much the same the job as the modest selection of lenses you might use with an SLR. A typical super-zoom will offer you 12x or 18x zoom, giving you a reasonable wide angle at the bottom end up to a pretty powerful telephoto at the top. Super-zooms also tend to offer a greater selection of settings options than regular compacts, giving you more flexibility over how you set up your photos.

The super-zoom is the answer for anyone who longs for extra telephoto power but doesn't want to buy an SLR and long lens. It won't break the bank, nor will it break your neck, even if you carry it around all day. If you are serious about your photography you may well start to become aware of the shortcomings of your super-zoom sooner or later. Common problems include noisy images at higher ISOs, camera shake at maximum zoom in all but the brightest conditions, and a disappointingly small range of aperture settings. If things like this start to bother you you'll probably start planning to invest in an SLR, but hang onto the super-zoom too if you can, its versatility and simplicity will continue to serve you well in all kinds of situations.

**FZ18 front**
Panasonic's DMC-FZ18 is an example of a super-zoom or 'bridge' camera – basically a beefed-up compact designed to offer some of the versatility of an SLR with its long zoom lens and comprehensive array of controls.

components, but even those from the best combination won't stand up alongside images taken on an SLR with a good lens. Most birdwatchers who digiscope use it as a way to take 'record shots' of what they see. However, it's an interesting and not too expensive (provided you already own a scope!) way to take extreme telephoto images. It's also possible to take photos through binoculars – they won't be very good photos, but if you have only a small compact and a pair of binoculars at hand, and the weird bird in your garden could fly off at any moment, before you have a chance to look it up in the book, they'll certainly be better than nothing.

**Digiscope set-up**
This is a more serious approach to digiscoping, with a purpose-built bracket holding the camera in line with the telescope's eyepiece and providing better stability, and therefore less camera shake.

# Settings and modes

### SHUTTER SPEED

This is the length of time that the aperture is open when you press the shutter. It works hand-in-hand with aperture to make sure your photos are correctly exposed. A longer shutter speed results in more light getting in, but also creates more chance of a blurry image, as your subject has more time to move, and your hands have more time to wobble (camera shake). If you are photographing something that doesn't move, and/or you use a tripod to eliminate camera shake, it's easier to use slower shutter speeds.

### DEPTH OF FIELD

This refers to how much of what you can see in the frame comes out in focus. If you are taking a photo of a seascape, and you want everything from the rocks in the foreground to the boat far out to sea to be in focus, you need a large depth of field. If you are photographing an insect on a flower and you want it to stand out from the masses of grass behind it, you need a shallow depth of field, with the background blurred away and free of distracting contrasts. While you can't tell the camera to use a particular depth of field, in general, the wider the aperture (the higher the f-number) and the shorter the focal length of the lens, the more depth of field you'll get.

### ISO SETTING

Camera film comes in a variety of ISO settings. Low ISO film, rated at 50 or 64, produces the finest images, with the clearest, most intense colours and least amount of graininess. However, it also needs the most light. In duller light conditions, the shutter speeds required to take an ISO 50 image are often impossibly slow. Higher ISO film (ratings range from 100-800 or even 1600) needs progressively less light to achieve fast enough shutter speeds for sharp images, but produces progressively grainier, duller images. Some digital cameras offer a range of ISO

**Grasshopper**
Focusing at close range can be critical and depends on the angle of photographer to subject and the aperture in use. Despite shooting this grasshopper at f16 (top photo), only the head and upper body is sharp as the subject is angled in such a way that the depth of field isn't great enough for it all to be in focus. Compare this to the photo below, taken at the same aperture but the photographer has moved slightly so the grasshopper is side-on.
*Nikon D300, Nikon 105mm macro lens, ISO 200, 1/160th sec at f16*

ratings, working the same way as with film, but you can change the ISO ratings from image to image if you want.

## WHITE BALANCE

One of the sensor's jobs is to try to convert 'real-world' light into a form that more closely matches what our eyes see. When we look at the world, our brains do this for us, automatically compensating for the colour casts caused by particular kinds of light. In a camera, you can tell the sensor how to adjust the image to allow for this. Many compact cameras have some simple white balance modes, such as 'bright sunlight', 'fluorescent light' and so on. SLRs have much finer white balance controls, allowing you to make small adjustments to 'colour temperature' to get just the right look.

## POINT AND SHOOT MODE

For almost all cameras, especially simpler ones, there is an automatic mode that enables you to pick up the camera, point it at your subject, press the shutter and take an acceptable image without doing anything to the camera's settings. In this mode, the camera automatically controls aperture, shutter speed, focus and (if the camera has it, and if it's required) flash. Without flash, it will choose the fastest shutter speed it can from the available light, which will usually mean the smallest aperture available, to freeze movement and reduce the chance of camera shake.

## APERTURE PRIORITY MODE

In this mode, you take some control and tell the camera what aperture you want it to use. It then automatically adjusts the shutter speed to whatever's required to make the image work with that aperture. You may use this mode when you want maximum depth of field, for which you'll need the widest aperture possible.

## SHUTTER SPEED PRIORITY MODE

In this mode, you set a particular shutter speed and let the camera choose the right aperture for that shutter speed. You might use this mode in low-light conditions or when using a heavy lens, when you want the fastest shutter speed you can get to eliminate camera shake.

## OTHER AUTOMATIC MODES

Some compacts have a selection of automatic modes designed for different types of photography, often designated by symbols. For example, an 'action' mode, indicated by a running person symbol perhaps, is likely to be a mode that automatically sets the fastest shutter speed possible to freeze a fast-moving subject and will adjust the other settings around this, while a 'landscape' mode will automatically set a wide aperture for maximum depth of field.

## METERING MODES

A camera's metering system takes a reading of light from the scene you're pointing it at, and from that it works out how best to expose the image. On most cameras, you can decide whether to take your light reading from a small point within the image (spot-metering) or from a more general area (average metering) – as usual, SLRs will give you more control than compacts. A spot-metering mode allows you to control how well the different parts of an image are exposed – pretty much essential to get exposure right in a highly contrasting image.

## EXPOSURE COMPENSATION

This feature allows you to adjust the exposure measured by your camera's light meter. Once you have half-pressed the shutter and the camera has done its metering and told you what aperture and shutter speed will be used for the photo, you can use the exposure compensation control to tell the camera to either over- or underexpose the image. It will then recalculate the shutter speed and aperture accordingly (or just one of them if you are in aperture priority or shutter speed priority mode). Usually, the range of adjustment goes from +2 to -2 in 1/3 steps. Exposure compensation is useful for when conditions are unusually dark, or very bright, such as snowy scenes.

# SLRs

The single-lens reflex camera, with its system of camera body plus interchangeable lenses, is the tool of choice for most professional wildlife photographers and a good many keen amateurs too. For every kind of SLR, there is a multitude of different lenses, all suitable for different kinds of photography, making the SLR a far more versatile choice than any compact. Also, SLRs tend to offer far better optics than compact cameras, and a greater range of settings and options. All this comes at a price, of course, and the more comprehensive your collection of lenses, and other accessories, the less likely you are to be able to lift it.

When you decide to invest in an SLR, think carefully about what kind of photographs you'll want to take – this will help you decide which lens or lenses to choose. For general wildlife photography, a zoom lens that takes you from a reasonable wide-angle to a modest telephoto length – say 24-70mm, or even 28-200mm – is a good start. For extra telephoto pulling power a longer zoom of 75-300mm, or 200-400mm, or a prime (fixed focal length) lens of anything between 300 and 600mm will cover most eventualities. If your interest lies in small subjects, a 90 or 100mm macro lens will be top of your shopping list.

**Cranefly**
This shot was taken on a digital SLR using a 105mm macro lens, which allows closer focusing than other types of lens. This female cranefly, or 'Daddy Longlegs', is laying its eggs. *Nikon D2X, Nikon 105mm lens, ISO 200, 1/1000th sec at f5.6*

Most telephoto lenses of 300mm and above have a maximum aperture of f4 or f5.6; anything wider than this gives you an extremely heavy – and very expensive – lens that would be virtually unusable in the field.

**D300**

The D300 is one of Nikon's professional-standard SLR cameras – a versatile and optically superb machine, ideal for the keen wildlife photographer.

## What make, what model?

Big camera manufacturers sell a range of SLRs, which scale up in price and sophistication as you'd expect. Their full range of lenses works with all of the different SLR models, so if you upgrade your camera body you won't need to replace your lenses – unless you switch manufacturers. For this reason, photographers tend to stay loyal to a single manufacturer once they've invested in some lenses – it's simply too expensive to switch.

Choosing a manufacturer is therefore an important and rather pressured choice when buying an SLR. There aren't that many to choose between; but they all have their advantages and disadvantages – it's quite possible to drive yourself insane weighing up

all the different factors. Independent reviewers are your friends here, but perhaps the best thing you can do is get some hands-on time with a few different cameras. Convince some photographer friends to let you have a play with their equipment. Alternatively, many retailers have 'field days' where you can try out a range of kit in the outdoors, at various nature reserves or country fairs. Often the 'feel' of a camera is either 'right', or 'wrong', in some intangible sense, and different models within a range tend to have the same 'feel'. A lot of money is at stake so it's worth taking your time. Conversely, beware of getting stuck in an eternal waiting game – there's always something better just around the corner and you can end up perpetually holding out for the next new model when the chances are that the perfect camera for you is already out there.

## Extras

These can be broadly divided into four categories – essentials, things to help you take photos, things to carry your stuff around in and things on which to store your digital images

### Don't leave home without it

Cameras are often power-hungry, so make sure you always have spare batteries with you – rechargeable ones are best. A lens cleaning cloth is another must, for keeping optics and view-screen free from dust and splashes. Also carry around your lens caps if they're not fixed to the camera or lenses, in case it rains. Camera kit is distressingly prone to fungus infestation, so you need to do all you can to keep your stuff dry.

### Tripods, converters and filters

Nothing shouts 'professional photographer at work' like a big lens mounted on a tripod. However, a tiny compact perched on top of that same tripod gives a rather different message – overkill. Street cred aside, you probably don't need to worry about buying a tripod unless you're using an SLR, though they can be handy for low-light landscape

shots with bigger compacts. The main purpose of the tripod is to hold your camera steady and thus eliminate camera shake at slow shutter speeds. The tripod can also help you to frame your shot; for example, some contain a spirit-level to help ensure you have a level horizon.

You are probably going to need a tripod that's nearly as tall as you are, so you can comfortably use it standing up. Heavier tripods are less likely to wobble or fall over in high winds than light ones, but that may well not be a factor in your garden. A pan-and-tilt head is relatively easy to use, but a ball-and-socket head allows you more flexibility in framing your photo.

A monopod gives a degree of stability while being more portable than a tripod. Another lightweight stability option is the bean bag – place bean bag on suitable surface and rest camera on bean bag. This does rely on your finding a wall, rock or similar at a suitable height, although the bean bag can be reshaped to control where your camera is pointing to a certain extent.

Teleconverters and filters fix to your lens to give you extra focal length, or to modify your image. They are mostly for SLRs, but some are made for super-zooms and compacts. Popular SLR teleconverters include 1.4x and 2x – they provide extra zoom but at the cost of reduced light reaching the sensor – you'll need more available light than usual. You can buy colour-graduated filters that give your images a colour tint, polarizing filters that reduce glare, improve contrast and cut out reflectivity (great for shots looking into still water), and macro filters that permit closer focusing.

Other kit you may fancy includes cable releases that enable you to take photos without touching the camera, external flash units that allow you to better control light levels, and lens hoods that help reduce lens flare (bright spots on your images) from sunshine.

## Camera bags

The best bag for your camera kit is the one that holds everything securely, allows easy access to it all, and is comfortable to lug around. Depending on your kit, that may be a simple neck pouch or a big, rugged rucksack. Choose something well padded, both as a whole, and within its various compartments, with enough space to hold everything you have now plus any kit you plan to add in the near future. Many larger camera bags have adjustable dividers to deal with any combination of SLR body/bodies and lenses with separate pouches for memory cards, spare batteries, lens cleaning cloth and so on. Even if your photographic forays are limited to your own garden, it's still worth buying a sturdy and waterproof kit bag.

## Image storage

One of the few givens about your camera, whatever it is, is that it won't have enough built-in memory for you. However, it will have a slot for you to insert a memory card, thus boosting the on-board memory and enabling you to take more photos at a time. Memory cards come in a range of sizes from a paltry 256MB to a whopping 32GB or more. Most SLR cameras use compact flash cards, and most compact cameras use SD cards, but a few use dedicated, manufacturer-specific cards. Check carefully what type your camera uses – very few cameras take more than one kind of memory card. Buy several and hang onto their little plastic cases to protect them from damage.

You'll probably store your photos on your home computer or laptop. For extra image storage, you could invest in a portable hard drive. This will interface with your computer (and perhaps also your camera) via a

**Robin singing**

Backing up your files is important; either burn copies of your best images to CDs/DVDs or copy them to a separate hard drive. There is nothing worse than taking a shot that you are totally happy with and have spent a long time over, such as this singing Robin, and then losing it because of computer or hard drive failure. It only takes seconds to back up files, but will take you an age to replace lost images.
*Nikon D2X, Sigma 300-800mm lens (at 700mm), ISO 200, 1/250th sec at f5.6*

USB cable. Such drives can be very capacious – 120-500GB are standard sizes. Some models are ultra light and portable; others have a view screen and simple interface so you can look at your photos on them.

CHAPTER **4** **Picture this**

**Bark of London Plane tree**
The natural world is brimming with subject material – train yourself to look for the beauty in the detail as well as at the bigger picture. London Plane trees are found in even the most industrialized settings, and their variegated bark is a treat to photograph.
*Panasonic DMC-FZ18, ISO 100, 1/500th sec at f6.3*

The beauty of the typical modern compact camera is that anyone can pick one up and take a reasonable photograph, but that's just the start. Your camera is a powerful and versatile tool, and so is your imagination. Add them together and the result will be amazing photos rather than simply average ones. This chapter deals with mastering the controls and settings of your camera, so you'll be able to make the very most of both planned and unexpected photo opportunities.

# Movement

As a wildlife photographer, you'll mostly be dealing with things that move around. Some of them move around a lot. It will often seem to you that they take particular delight in moving away very fast the moment you pick up your camera.

That's just one of the frustrations of this hobby, but the other side of the coin is that with a camera you can capture moments that come and go too quickly to even really register in the eye. Remember that it wasn't until the first photographs were taken of galloping horses that we realized that they never have all their legs outstretched at the same moment, as was popularly shown in 18th century paintings.

So with the camera you can freeze a moment lasting 1/2,000 of a second or even less. You can also go the other way, and record longer exposures of a second or more, which will show movement (if there is any) as it happens rather than eliminate it. Varying your shutter speed gives you lots of options for creative photography.

**Woodpigeon** (right)
Flying birds will test your patience to the limit, but at least with a digital camera there is no wasted film. The camera can freeze movement that the eye will never see, allowing the bird's details to be studied later.
*Nikon D2X, Sigma 300-800mm lens (at 650mm), ISO 200, 1/1600th sec at f5.6*

**Starlings bathing** (below)
Using slow shutter speeds for wildlife photography usually results in blurred images; but on some occasions this can be an effective way of showing movement in your images. This flock of bathing Starlings was taken at 1/100 of a second at f11 aperture and the result is quite pleasing; shooting at f5.6 would have meant the shutter speed would have been almost 1/500 of a second, which would have frozen much of the movement.
*Nikon D1X, Nikon 800mm lens, ISO 200, 1/100th sec at f11*

## Shutter speeds and ISO

In many cases, you're going to want to use the quickest shutter speed you can. Birds move around very quickly, and small insects get buffeted by even the slightest breeze. Faster shutter speeds also reduce the chances of an image being spoilt by camera shake. With shutter speeds slower than 1/60th of a second, you're likely to start seeing a bit of camera shake blur, and the problem gets worse in heavier cameras with bigger lenses. Most point-and-shoot modes will give you a shutter speed fast enough to freeze motion in the current light settings if they possibly can, or you can use shutter priority mode and set the fastest shutter speed that you can – the camera will compensate for this by making the aperture wider (a lower f-number), so more light can get in during the short exposure.

If you're struggling with low light, you can give yourself some extra 'wiggle room' on shutter speed by changing the ISO rating. Doubling the ISO rating halves the exposure time you need to record the scene at the same aperture – for example, if an exposure of 1/250 of a second at f8 is required at ISO 100, then at ISO 200 you can take the same photo in 1/500 of a second at f8, and at ISO 400, in 1/1,000 of a second at f8. Be aware that the image will be noisier at higher ISOs. If you're already going to have noise issues – for example you're working at the extreme telephoto end of a compact zoom lens – you may find that anything above ISO 100 gives you impossible levels of noise. However, noisiness is not always a bad thing. The grainy look of a photo with some noise can be quite atmospheric, working best in images that are stronger on contrast than they are on colour.

To record a moving element in an otherwise static scene – say, flowering grass heads waving in the breeze, or a whirling flock of Starlings against a dramatic sky – you can use the shutter priority mode to set a long shutter exposure – the camera will choose a suitable aperture to go with it (or warn you if light conditions mean that even the smallest aperture will overexpose the image at that shutter speed). You'll probably need an exposure of a second or more to capture meaningful movement, which means you'll need to stabilize the camera somehow, so you don't spoil the effect by adding extra movement in the form of camera shake. A tripod is ideal but you can just place the camera on a solid surface. Get the image framed and focused as you wish, then use the camera's self-timer to take the photo automatically, ensuring you don't introduce a wobble by pressing the shutter button.

**Nuthatch**
By changing the ISO setting to 800 it was possible to use a shutter speed of 1/60th of a second, which was just enough to stop movement (and camera shake), as this Nuthatch paused briefly on a branch. If the ISO had been left on 200 the exposure would have been a slow 1/15th of a second, resulting in a totally blurred image.
*Nikon D2X, Sigma 300-800mm lens (at 800mm), ISO 800, 1/60th sec at f5.6*

# Bursting with ideas

Most cameras have a 'burst mode', which means the camera will take a series of shots in very rapid succession (several per second), rather than just one, when you press the shutter. This mode, coupled with fast shutter speeds, is great for tackling a busy, fast-changing scene where things are happening too quickly for you to be able to compose the image just as you want it. Use a big memory card and take lots of shots, and you might catch just the one you want or, more likely, something completely unexpected but very interesting nonetheless.

**Starlings**
Two for the price of one – but the chances of catching both Starlings in pleasing poses were considerably less than they would be for one on its own. The burst mode is tailor-made for opportunities like this.
*Panasonic DMC-FZ18, ISO 100, 1/500th sec at f8*

**Great Tit**
Don't put the camera away in bad weather; as long as you and your equipment are dry just carry on taking pics. This image of a Great Tit on a sleety, wet, dull, miserable day was taken by using ISO 1,600 at 1/80th of a second. The slower shutter speed has just about got the bird sharp, but the falling sleet is blurred into streaks, and the bird looks as miserable as the weather was.
*Nikon D300, Sigma 300-800mm lens (at 800mm), ISO 1600, 1/80th sec at f5.6*

# Depth of field

Here's another element which you can manipulate to radically alter the impression your images give. In every photo, there is a distance from the camera – or 'depth' – within which everything will be in 'perfect' focus. Everything closer to, and further away from, that plane of perfect focus is less sharply focused, but the rate of focus loss, relative to distance from the perfect depth, varies according to shutter speed and aperture. Slow shutter speeds, at narrow apertures (high f-numbers), produce images with greater depth of field – near objects look just as sharp as distant ones. The fast shutter speed/wide aperture (low f-number) combination produces a shallow depth of field, the objects at the perfect focal point standing out clearly from a blurred foreground and background. The latter is often best for wildlife photographs, which is why professional wildlife photographers often use very big, very heavy telephoto lenses that go down to f4 (for a 500mm lens), or f2.8 (for a 300mm lens).

**Magpie**

This photo, and the one above, were taken at exactly the same exposure, 1/500th of a second at f5.6, but, as the focus point on the above image was the bird's head only, the shallow depth of field results in the lower body and tail being outside the depth of focus. In the lower image the whole bird is in focus as it is side-on and all of it is within the narrow plane of focus.
*Nikon D300, Sigma 300-800mm lens (at 650mm), ISO 200, 1/500th sec at f5.6*

Sometimes a combination of low light and a lively subject mean that you don't really have much choice about depth of field – it's going to be a narrow one, and unless your subject is a fairly flat creature like a butterfly, you may well find that not all of it is in focus. In cases like this, try to focus on your subject's eye, or eyes (if it has obvious eyes!) and you may still come away with photos with impact, even if the subject is partly blurred.

Landscape photographers use slow shutter speeds a lot, to record as much depth of field as possible, and to capture the low, but often delicious, light of very early mornings, or late evenings. You may find the same trick helpful in the smaller-scale landscape of your garden, or for still-life shots of a collection of small objects.

SLR cameras invariably give you a wider range of shutter speeds and aperture settings than compacts do, and different SLR lenses vary in this respect as well – it can be very difficult to get much depth of field through a long telephoto lens, for example. You'll get the best shots by working within the limits of your camera, but you'll need to experiment with different subjects in different lighting conditions to find out your particular camera's strengths and weaknesses.

### Daffodils

Okay, this is not your average garden, it has to be said… but if you get the chance to visit any country estates, take the camera. Using a wide-angle lens, a low viewpoint and f13 aperture has enabled this entire image to be in focus, emphasizing the early flowering of daffodils against a winter backdrop of leafless trees.

*Nikon D2X, Sigma 18-50mm lens (at 18mm), ISO 200, 1/200th sec at f13*

**Four-spotted Chaser dragonfly**
With close-ups of large insects, you'll often want to
focus on their eyes, although other parts of them can
be interesting too.
*Nikon D300, Nikon 105mm macro lens, ISO 200,
1/60th sec at f8*

# Focus

The conventional wisdom on focusing is straightforward. Your subject should be in focus. If the subject is an animal with recognizable facial features, its eyes in particular should be in focus. The other elements in the frame don't need to be sharp – in fact, if they will potentially distract from the subject, then they should not be. If the whole frame is the subject, for example in a landscape shot, then the whole frame should be in focus.

Camera autofocus makes an educated (to a greater or lesser extent) guess about what you want to be in focus, depending on where you are pointing the camera, but it's far from infallible. However, the results of autofocus mishaps can be successes in their own right, and can spawn ideas for new and imaginative images. Perhaps you're photographing a flock of House Sparrows feeding on the lawn, or a gathering of snails on top of your wall. Your first thought might be to try to get as many individuals in focus as possible. Your next thought might be to focus on the nearest individuals and let the more distant ones blur into the background. However, focusing on a subject midway between front and back could also make an interesting image, with more of a sense of depth than the previous two ideas.

Let's say that after a spell in the hide you're rewarded with a chance at a frame-filling portrait of a Red Fox drinking at your pond, but you can't get the animal's whole face in focus because the light is bad and you're using a long lens. By all means focus on the eyes, but try a few shots with the focus on the nose and tongue too – you might catch some nice sharp water droplets and tell a more meaningful story. It's essential to master your camera's manual focus control for times when you want to do something a bit unconventional with focusing.

# Close-up

The majority of the animals living in your garden are very small and easily overlooked. If you're going to go to the trouble of searching them out, you'll want to make sure your photos can do them justice, and in most cases that means you'll need some kind of macro lens. Many compacts have a macro mode, which allows closer focusing than the standard mode. You'll find this works better at the short end of the zoom range than at higher magnifications. For SLRs, specific macro lenses are available. These typically have a focal length of around 100mm, go down to f2.8 and will give you the best – and biggest – results, allowing you to take life-size photos of small animals without having to get extremely close to them. You can also achieve close focusing with the use of a macro filter, or (on an SLR) with extension rings, or bellows, that fit between the camera and the lens.

**Garden Carpet**
Quality of digital compacts can be excellent, and their close-focus capabilities can sometimes match, or even better, that of a very expensive macro lens on a digital SLR. Compare these two moth photographs – a Garden Carpet and a Willow Beauty – and see which was taken with the compact. *Nikon D1X, Nikon 105mm macro lens, ISO 200, 1/30th sec at f8*

Unless you have a macro lens, you will probably need to move the camera very close to your subject animal to get a reasonably large image of it in the frame. This action will spook many flying insects, but persevere – sometimes you will find the one among the many that tolerates a very close approach. To improve your chances, always approach your subjects very slowly and carefully (these animals' eyes are optimized to spot movement rather than recognize the dreaded human form) and be especially careful that your shadow, and that of your camera, does not fall across your subject, as this is likely to scare it off (and if it doesn't, the shadow will still spoil your photo). Most flying insects are more sluggish when the weather is cooler, so try searching for them early in the morning. Butterflies often spend time basking with wings spread at first, and last, light, to make the most of the sun's warmth. This can be a great time to photograph them.

**Willow Beauty**
*Panasonic DMC-FZ18, ISO 100, 1/100th sec at f8*

**Painted Lady side-on**
It is the same butterfly in both photos, taken using the same exposure, but different angles have given strikingly different results.
*Nikon D2X, Nikon 105mm macro lens, ISO 200, 1/250th sec at f11*

**Painted Lady head-on**
*Nikon D2X, Nikon 105mm macro lens, ISO 200, 1/250th sec at f11*

# Alternate viewpoints

With macro photography it can be difficult to achieve a good depth of field. For this reason (and because some photographers lack imagination) the vast majority of the photos you'll see of insects and other small animals are taken from above, looking down onto the animal's back, which tends to be the way you see these creatures in real life. Taking this approach will give you clear, straightforward images, and is especially good for large-winged insects that rest with their wings stretched wide open – butterflies, dragonflies and so on. You may, however, want to get a bit more adventurous and try some different camera angles for your macro shots. Instead of top-down, try head-on for example. It may not be possible to identify your subject animal from the resultant photo, or even recognize it as an inhabitant of planet Earth, but it will give you a striking new perspective.

**Home-made reflector**

When you're photographing insects or plants in close-up, you will often encounter situations where you want to manipulate the direction and intensity of natural light conditions a little to improve your image. A square of foil stuck to a card makes a handy portable reflector, which you can use to bounce some extra light onto the more shadowed parts of the picture. For example, you can place your reflector on the ground below the plant you're photographing to light up the lower parts of the foliage. The reflector can also be a useful tool in manipulating insect behaviour. If you find a butterfly resting with its wings closed on a dull day, and you want to photograph it with wings open, you may be able to induce it to spread its wings by reflecting light onto it to fool it into believing the sun is about to come out.

**Small Copper a**

Take different types of images of the same subject, to give yourself fresh challenges and look at different ways of taking an image. The first image, photo a, is a standard closed-wing close-up portrait of a Small Copper butterfly, while photo b sets the butterfly in context within its habitat. Photo c is a different take on the subject – the angle makes the butterfly nearly unidentifiable to a species, but it is still a striking shot.

*Nikon D300, Nikon 105mm macro lens, ISO 200, 1/125th sec at f16*

**Small Copper b**

*Nikon D300, Nikon 105mm macro lens, ISO 200, 1/125th sec at f16*

## Back off

If your camera's macro capabilities are limited, that doesn't necessarily mean you can't take good photos of small creatures. You can simply step back a bit and pay more attention to the stuff that will occupy the rest of the frame. Showing an animal as an element within its habitat can be just as rewarding as a full-frame portrait with no obvious context. Photos of small animals en masse can also be dramatic, looking at first glance like textural abstracts but on closer examination revealing a whole mini-world of action.

Look for colours, textures and patterns that go well with the animal subject – or contrast with it in arresting ways. When you're out and about, you might want to collect interesting 'props' – feathers, pine cones, attractive pebbles and so on – to scatter about your garden in places where photographable invertebrates may be found. If there are obvious signs of your subject's interactions with its environment, they can be included (for example, a caterpillar surrounded by the skeletons of the leaves it's been eating). Backing away a bit should enable you to achieve a greater depth of field, thus ensuring both subject and surroundings are in focus.

**Small Copper c**

*Nikon D300, Nikon 105mm macro lens, ISO 200, 1/125th sec at f16*

# Natural light

Once you start getting interested in photography, you'll acquire a whole new appreciation for the range of lighting conditions that may be observed in the outdoor world. No longer are days divided simply into 'morning', 'afternoon' and 'night', or weather into just 'sunny' or 'raining'. You'll find the light to be just as capricious as the animals themselves when taking wildlife photos – as with animals, the more familiar you become with the normal behaviour of light, the better you'll be able to predict what it's going to do and when.

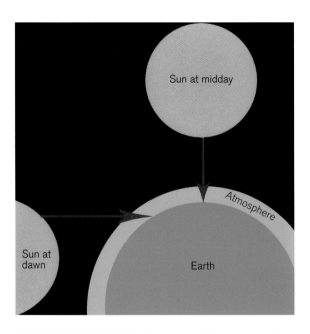

## Colour temperature

Sunlight and most artificial light is more or less 'white light', which (you'll remember from school) can be split into the full colour spectrum if you shine it through a prism. The objects around us absorb some of that light and reflect back the rest – so blue objects look blue because they absorb all the colours in white light apart from the blue, which is reflected back at us. If we use an artificial light source that isn't white but coloured, the colours of the objects it shines on are distorted, to our eyes.

Sunlight is at its whitest at midday; however, early and late in the day it becomes redder and warmer. This is because the Earth's atmosphere absorbs some of the blue light in sunlight, and at dawn and dusk the sunlight has to get through a thicker layer of atmosphere, because it is coming from a lower angle (see diagram above). As a result, everything looks warmer, rosier and more yellow at dawn and dusk – this is particularly noticeable in the clouds that form colourful sunrises and sunsets.

For you, the photographer, this means that the colours of your subjects often look richer, more intense and more glowing in early or late sunlight than they do in the middle of the day, especially as warm-spectrum colours tend to dominate in the natural world. However, light levels are also lower overall at these times, which will of course affect the shutter speeds you can use.

## Light direction

The angle of the sun relative to the Earth affects the sizes of the shadows that objects cast – the lower the sun, the longer the shadows, and when the light is right overhead there are hardly any shadows to be seen. At the extremes of the day, the sun only hits the highest points around, and the shadows of land contours plunge large areas into shade. Light coming in from the side also creates dramatic contrasts on the features of an individual animal – this can be good or bad, depending on your aims for the photograph and the exact direction of the light. Strong midday light is good for guaranteeing you fast shutter speeds, but can produce rather flat and lifeless-looking images.

Where you position yourself relative to your subject, and to the sun, will affect how your subjects look. Traditional photographic wisdom says that you should place yourself in between subject and light source for an evenly lit image. However, positioning the subject between you and the light produces a backlit subject, which can make for an attractive photo in some cases. Backlighting can produce a 'halo effect', or 'rim lighting', whereby the animal's 'outside edge', for want of a better term, is lit up. This is particularly striking in furry animals, where the 'halo' of light catches the individual hairs. Obviously there's a whole swathe of middle ground between strongly front-lit and strongly backlit views – plenty of scope for you to experiment and see what results you like best.

**Song Thrush**

The dappled light shining through the trees and falling on to the back of this Song Thrush has made for a pleasing image, although the shade the bird was sitting in has meant a shutter speed of only 1/80 of a second was used.

*Nikon D2X, Sigma 300-800mm lens (at 390mm), ISO 200, 1/80th sec at f5.6*

**Song Thrush backlit**

Light from behind a subject can change the natural colour that you would expect, but the effects can be pleasing. The grass looks more of a pastel shade than 'real' grass. Exposure may be difficult, so take a few shots at different settings.

*Nikon D2X, Sigma 300-800mm lens (at 650mm), ISO 200, 1/100th sec at f5.6*

**Blue Tit side-lit/backlit**

The sun shining from the left and towards the back of this Blue Tit has bleached out the willow bud blossoms, leaving them as almost white blobs. But it is a nice effect and adds to the finished photo as a spring image. Spot metering was used to take a reading from the Blue Tit itself to ensure a correct exposure.

*Nikon D1X, Nikon 500mm lens, ISO 200, 1/160th sec at f5.6*

## Weather

For some photographers, a cloudy sky means stay at home and don't even attempt to take any photos. When the rain starts to fall, there's even less incentive to get out there – raindrops on your lens will not make for good photos, even if you do manage to get enough light into the camera to take any.

Less than sunny weather is not necessarily a disaster, though. The loss of light on cloudy days may place serious restrictions on telephoto photography, which depends on good light to achieve acceptable shutter speeds, but don't rule it out altogether. Hazy sunshine or bright but cloudy days can be fine for long-lens work, and the lack of strong contrast can be an advantage for all kinds of photography.

Rain goes hand in hand with low light so the problems of shutter speed will still be with you. However, if you're using a shorter lens, or photographing static subjects, you can take some great – and unconventional – photos in the rain. Some

**Sallow Kitten** (above)
Some subjects are better photographed in duller light; this Sallow Kitten moth, a species found in many gardens, was photographed after being attracted to a moth-trap overnight. The light was dull but this has helped to retain detail in the white markings and the patterns of the scales on its wings.
*Nikon D1X, Nikon 105mm macro lens, ISO 200, 1/60th sec at f8*

**Redwing** (opposite, below)
It's easy to be put off by dull weather – but if your time to take photos is limited, it is worth persevering and trying anyway. This Redwing was taken at 1/40 of a second – although many images taken at this slow speed will be ruined by camera shake it is worth the effort for the sharp one.
*Nikon D2X, Sigma 300-800mm lens (at 600mm), ISO 320, 1/40th sec at f5.6*

animals come into their own when the rain starts to fall – snails literally come out of their shells, and many birds enjoy 'bathing' in falling rain. You'll need to shelter your lens from rain splashes, so ideally you'll be in a hide or under some kind of cover.

**Mistle Thrush tugging worm**
(above)
Wet weather is perfect for certain images, as long as the equipment is kept dry. Rain will soften the ground, and bring worms nearer the surface, meaning birds like this Mistle Thrush will be out hunting.
*Nikon D200, Sigma 300-800mm lens (at 480mm), ISO 200, 1/160th sec at f5.6*

If your garden receives one of the UK's increasingly rare snowfalls, you're probably going to want to record the event, and hopefully capture some of your garden wildlife against the pristine white backdrop. Snow creates a challenge from the lighting point of view – on the one hand it provides reflected light from below, which can give an interesting new look to animals walking across it, but on the other it is difficult to expose correctly and often comes out a dull grey colour, rather than pristine white, especially on cloudy days. This happens when your camera interprets the snow as bright lighting and so underexposes it. Some cameras have a special 'snow mode'. Otherwise, you can get the exposure right by spot-metering from a bright patch of snow, then using your camera's exposure compensation to increase the exposure by +1 or +2.

**Magpie in snow** (above)

Spot metering was again used in this shot, a reading taken from the small area of uncovered grass. If your camera does not have spot metering then take a reading from a snow-free area, such as a tree trunk, and expose for that. Failing this expose for the snow but compensate by dialling in at least +1 or maybe even +2 on the exposure dial. Check the screen to see if the exposure is correct or take a few images at different exposures.

*Nikon D300, Sigma 300-800mm lens (at 480mm), ISO 400, 1/1000th sec at f5.6*

**Snowdrops** (right)

Using a wide-angle lens and a low angle to take this image has led to a pleasing shot; a meter reading was taken from the green stems of the Snowdrops.

*Nikon D2X, Sigma 18-50mm lens (at 24mm), ISO 200, 1/250th sec at f16*

**Garden Spider**
A small burst of flash has lit this spider, but not reached the background which is natural light. It is important to experiment with your own flashgun's settings to see what works and what doesn't. Too much flash at close range will bleach out the subject while not enough will render it very dark. Digital is a perfect tool for this experimentation as it is possible to see what is happening immediately after each image has been taken.
*Nikon D2X, Nikon 105mm macro lens, ISO 200, 1 /100th sec at f16, SB800 flash, on manual setting; set to -1/3rd*

# Flash

Camera flash can help to brighten up a dull image or even out a very contrasting one. However, it is all too often a good example of using a sledgehammer to crack a nut – a burst of artificial light can transform a slightly too gloomy scene into a horrendously overexposed and glaring mess. For the wildlife photographer, striving to capture a natural outdoors scene, flash should be used with particular care.

As with so many things, a cheaper camera is going to have a simple built-in flash unit, which sits close to the lens and has few options for modifying the way it works. A super-zoom or SLR is likely to have pop-up flash, a larger and more versatile flash unit which sits further from the lens. Built-in flash of any kind is only going to be effective when your subject is pretty close to you – around 3–5 metres depending on the type of flash. Most higher-end cameras have the means to attach external flash units, and the average professional SLR set-up for portrait photography will include several different external flashguns to provide light from a variety of directions. Wildlife photographers have less need for flash than photographers whose work is studio-based. In any case, whatever kit you have, your best bet is to get used to the way your camera works with the flash switched off (if your camera has a function that will let you do this) as overuse of flash will wreck many a potentially good image.

**To flash or not to flash**

As mentioned above, flash is pointless for a distant subject; however, fill-in flash can make all the difference in closer shots, whether they be bird photos taken from a hide, or macro shots. Experiment with flash settings when you have a compliant and reasonably 'easy' subject – a resting moth, a plant or even a still-life are all good. Shiny, smooth-surfaced subjects tend not to look great when photographed with flash – the reflections can be very harsh and glaring – and this unfortunately applies to many insects, such as beetles and ants. Some photographers get around this problem by using a flash diffuser that fits over the flash unit and softens the light it produces. Diffusers are made of translucent materials (often cloth or plastic) and come in a variety of styles. You can also make your own – try fixing a square of white tissue over the flash with a rubber band (easier on a pop-up flash).

Another point to bear in mind about flash is the ethics of using it to photograph nocturnal animals. A flash going off in your face is an unpleasant experience even when you know that it's coming, so imagine how alarming it must be for an animal that's happily going about its business and at perfect ease in the darkness. If you are serious about wanting to photograph owls, badgers, hedgehogs and so on at night, it is a good idea to try to use a separate permanent light source as well, which the animals can become accustomed to, and which will enable you to get your shots without using lots of flash.

# Types of flash

## AUTOMATIC FLASH

With this mode activated, the flash fires a full-strength burst as you press the shutter, whenever the camera detects that the available light is insufficient for a steady hand-held shot. It does this irrespective of whether whatever you're focusing on is within the range of the flash, so the result is often an extremely brightly lit immediate foreground and a background that recedes into total darkness. You will almost certainly want to turn this mode off.

## RED-EYE REDUCTION

To eliminate the dreaded 'red eye', caused by light reflected back from the retinas of the subject's eyes when the pupils are enlarged in low light, this flash mode fires a series of short 'dummy flashes' before the real flash goes off as the photo is taken. This has the effect of causing the subject's pupils to contract so less light can be reflected back. Its value in wildlife photography is negligible.

## FILL-IN FLASH

Now we're talking. This provides a more subtle and sophisticated way to use flash than the full-on 'flash on' mode, supplying only enough flash necessary for the lighting conditions and thus producing more natural-looking results. It is especially good at coping with backlighting, where you are photographing your subject against the sun or a brightly lit background. The camera's metering system provides an appropriate level of flash to fill in foreground shadows, so you don't end up with your subject in silhouette. (Of course, sometimes that will be exactly what you want to end up with, depending on the kind of photo you have in mind.)

**SLOW SYNCH** This mode, also known as night portrait mode, enables you to use flash in conjunction with a slow shutter speed, which will give more natural-looking lighting in very low-light settings. As with slow shutter speeds generally, you'll need to stabilize the camera with a tripod, or equivalent. The camera's metering system selects a slow shutter speed that correctly exposes a dark background using the available light, but also fires a fill-in flash at the end of the exposure to light up the foreground and freeze any motion that is going on in that foreground. This mode can produce very interesting (though sometimes rather weird) low-light or night-time shots.

# CHAPTER 5 Setting the scene

**Common Blue butterfly**

A simple picture, but effective and one that can be taken in many gardens with an area of weeds or long grass; the sort of habitat loved by Common Blues.

*Nikon D300, Nikkor 105mm macro lens, ISO 200, 1/125th sec at f16*

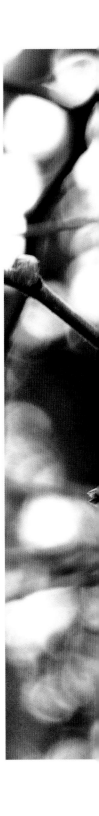

Close your eyes and think of a great wildlife photo – either a real one that you know, or one you'd love to see, or take yourself, some day. What's going on in the picture? It could be a crystal-clear moment of high drama, an impressive face-to-face portrait, or an abstract riot of pattern and colour. It could freeze a moving animal in an elegant or bizarre posture, or express motion as a blurring swirl. It might be a frame-filling shot of a glittering amphibian eye, or it could show an animal dwarfed by a huge landscape. Whatever you see, the chances are that the making of such an image involves planning, care and plenty of errors, each one with its own lesson to teach. Don't be afraid to make mistakes, break the rules and experiment with ideas – this is your chance to really throw yourself into the detail and magic of the image itself.

# Composition

If you're a paints-and-brushes artist, you can bend reality a little, or a lot, to make sure that every element in your painting is attractive and appropriate, and that they work together in a harmonious way, or an arresting way, or however you want them to. No such luck for the photographer – your options are limited to the different ways you can look at a real scene. However, making a perfect image out of messy reality takes more artistic feeling than you might realize.

## The rules and breaking them

Here are some of the classic rules of photographic composition, how and why they work, and when and why you might want to break them.

**The rule of thirds** To understand this rule, mentally divide up the frame of your image with two equally spaced horizontal lines and two equally spaced vertical lines, turning your frame into a grid of nine equal-sized rectangles, with four cross-over points around the centre of the frame. The rule of thirds states that, for a harmonious composition, you should frame your picture in a way that reflects this grid. So your horizon should be along one of these horizontal lines, not dead centre, and any dominant vertical elements should be at the one-third across or two-thirds across lines, not halfway across. Most importantly, place your object or objects of interest on, or very near, one or more of the four line cross-points. Positioning the subject a little off-centre gives it enough space around it to not look cramped, but also invites the eye to explore the frame of the photograph in a way that a subject placed dead centre does not.

Obeying this rule does produce reliably pleasing images. However, sometimes you will want to move your subject closer to the edge to give it a greater sense of its place as an entity existing with and dependent on its surroundings. If you are photographing an abstract subject, there may be no obvious features to place on the cross-points. And the centrally placed subject can have dramatic impact too, especially if it is large in the frame.

**Blue Tit**
The rule of thirds – the shape of the twigs provides the top
and right intersections, while the Blue Tit is positioned roughly
on the bottom left intersection point.
*Panasonic DMC-FZ18, ISO 100, 1/160th sec at f4*

**Make eye-contact** If you photograph an animal, you want it to be looking straight at the lens. The eye contact will make an engaging image. However, this isn't always possible. With mammals, and to a lesser extent birds, we can generally tell pretty easily whether there is eye contact going on, but it's not so easy with reptiles, amphibians and fish, and becomes almost impossible with insects and other invertebrates, so different are their eyes from ours. Sometimes a photograph can work well when the subject animal is looking at something else within the frame. When we look at someone who isn't looking at us, we instinctively follow their gaze to see why whatever it is they're looking at is more interesting than us. The same goes with animals – we might follow the fox's gaze and find the frog it's watching, or we might trace the path of a Sparrowhawk's gaze into the garden it's scanning for breakfast.

**Your subject should look into the frame** If your subject is off-centre, it should be facing into the larger space within the frame, rather than in the direction that's closer to the frame's edge. This follows on from the rule above – if

we're following an animal's gaze, we don't want that gaze to lead us straight out of the frame – we need a reason to look into the rest of the image. This rule is a hard one to break, but one way to do it is to have the rest of the image point towards the subject, rather than vice versa, so that the viewer finds the way to the subject via the other elements in the frame.

**Red Fox a** (above)
Rule of thirds – imagination or just plain wrong? This panoramic image of a fox hunting prey as it trots along allows the reader to follow the fox's eye-line into and then out of the frame.
*Nikon D2X, Sigma 300-800mm lens (at 800mm), ISO 200, 1/800th sec at f7.1*

**Red Fox b** (opposite)
A more standard shot with the fox facing into the camera, but both this and the first photo work – it all depends on your own preference.
*Nikon D2X, Sigma 300-800mm lens (at 700mm), ISO 200, 1/800th sec at f8*

**Fill the frame with your subject** It's a photo of a dragonfly, so the frame should be mostly occupied by the dragonfly, right? Not necessarily. It's not always possible to achieve this, depending on your optical limitations. Moreover, even if your lens is up to the job of frame-filling portraits, it can be good to step back a little, or a lot, to show your subject as just one element of a wider scene. If the surroundings are photogenic enough to warrant it, shots of animals 'in context' can often be more striking that the frame-fillers.

**Make a path through the frame** Make use of natural lines and curves in the frame to lead your viewer along a clear but winding path into and through the image. This can be an actual path or an implied one – your garden path itself or a linear pattern formed by light falling through the trees, or any of countless other possibilities. The eye naturally finds and follows contrasting edges – you can use this tendency to enhance a sense of depth and to lead the viewer to the elements of interest within a photo.

As with the rule of thirds, following this one will naturally produce pleasing images. However, bending or breaking it can produce arresting results. Try using crisscrossing or overlapping paths, or do away with paths altogether for a more abstract composition. Jarring elements and chaotic contrast patterns can be dramatic, perhaps enhanced and pulled together by including a single coherent element – a Blackbird feeding on a mass of red berries, or a white moth resting on the scratched and pitted bark of a tree.

**Common Darter** (above)
If you cannot get close enough for frame-filling images of your subject then sometimes including habitat and surroundings with the subject positioned nicely in the frame can be very effective. Using a longer lens or standing further back with a smaller one can also put a nervous subject at ease.
*Nikon D2X, Nikon 300mm lens, ISO 200, 1/200th sec at f16*

**Blue-tailed Damselfly** (opposite, above)
If you're photographing a small creature against a confusing backdrop of vegetation, try to include some linear elements. The long lines of grass blades and stems help give coherence to this Blue-tailed Damselfly shot.
*Panasonic DMC-FZ18, ISO 100, 1/250th sec at f5.6*

**Wood Ants** (opposite, below)
With a seething mass of animal life, like this busy Wood Ant nest, sometimes you can make a more interesting image by just filling the frame with chaotic action, over which the viewer's eye can roam, rather than trying to pick out a definite subject.
*Panasonic DMC-FZ18, ISO 100, 1/100th sec at f3.6*

**Shoot with the light behind you** Colours can go haywire when you look into the sun, hence the oft-quoted advice to position yourself between the sun and your subject for every photo. This will give you solid, and straightforward, colour representation and colour detail, but don't dismiss the alternatives out of hand. Shooting into the light might take away colour and detail, but it compensates for this by giving you much more contrast and, potentially, drama – a good thing, given the right subject and careful use of your light meter. Strong light coming in from the side can also make interesting photos, giving your subjects real solidity and depth.

**Brimstone**

The dull, flat light falling on to this Brimstone butterfly meant that no distracting shadows were thrown as they would have been on a sunny day. A combination of a slower shutter speed and a wider aperture had to be used, but the butterfly was fairly inactive anyway in the dull, cool conditions so the shot worked well.
*Nikon D300, Nikkor 105mm macro lens, ISO200, 1/200th sec at f9*

# Bringing the animal into the picture

Let's say you have determined that the animal you want to photograph is living in, or visiting, your garden. You've gone on to dream up, find or create a potential-packed backdrop for your chosen subject. Your next task is to convince the animal to step into the frame and pose for you –

how do you do this? It's difficult enough with pets and children, so how much worse must it be with wild animals? Needless to say, there are no guarantees. However, depending on the creature, there are a number of things you can do to help make your photo happen.

**All the comforts of home**

If your 'set' comprises the right habitat, your animal may well show up of its own accord, or be there already. As discussed in Chapter 3, think about the photos you want to take when you design, and create or modify, the elements of your garden. Your woodpile will attract foraging Wrens, so make sure it is a nice-looking woodpile. Damselflies will rest on foliage around your pond, so plant attractive foliage and make sure you have a good line of sight to it with no distracting elements in the backgrounds of the best views.

**Baiting**

Food is a great motivator for wild animals. Most of them spend hours of their daily (or nightly) routine searching for their next meal, so they are very good at it. They will often be very quick to discover new sources of food and won't waste any time wondering who put it there. If you want to find a more natural photographic setting for the birds that are already visiting your bird table and feeders, use your imagination to hide extra food in ways that the birds will see, but the camera won't: peanut butter spread on branches, nuts wedged into tree-bark cracks or seeds stuck to elegant dead flower-heads – your imagination is the limit.

Spraying a sugar solution onto tree leaves can attract a variety of insects. Various species of moth, butterflies and other insects feed naturally on something similar in the form of the 'honeydew' that aphids excrete as they consume leaves through the summer. Another time-honoured moth attractant is a heady brew of beer, molasses and other sweetly pungent substances, boiled up to a dark paste and painted onto tree trunks.

**Wren**
Wrens like to hunt insects, insects like to hide and live in woodpiles, so it makes sense to make a woodpile of your own; it may work and you won't know until you try.
*Nikon D2X, Sigma 300-800mm lens (at 750mm), ISO 200, 1/125th sec at f5.6*

If you have foxes visiting your garden, you can persuade them to linger by scattering around small morsels of meaty food, like dog or cat food. They'll take longer to locate all the titbits than they would if you presented food all in one place, so you'll have longer to take pictures – also, the food morsels will be inconspicuous so won't spoil your photos.

Mice and voles will willingly hoover up any nuts, seeds, peanut butter or dried fruit you leave out for them. Start by leaving the bait in concealed spots to help your guests feel safe, then gradually bait them into your photographic set. They will forage at dusk and dawn in the summer so you should be able to get well-lit photos if you're patient. They are capable climbers, so try baiting the lower branches of shrubs for some interesting alternative angles.

### Hand-made pictures

Some small animals are slow enough and/or fearless enough that you can physically move them into your composition. This is not to be undertaken lightly. The moment you pick up an animal, you are responsible for its well-being, and you must treat it with every care, before you return it to a safe place when you have taken photos.

When preparing a 'set' for photographing a small animal, think about including attractive 'props' and removing distracting or unattractive ones. A polished-looking beetle will be set off well against a ridged slab of decaying wood, while a delicate mayfly will look great resting on an equally delicate seeding grass head. Nicely patterned insects will often look very good on a relatively plain backdrop, like a smooth leaf or stone. For more complex compositions, you could use natural bits and pieces like fallen leaves, feathers or seed husks, perhaps to make a 'still life with not-so-still centipede'. Don't be afraid to include man-made props – house bricks, scrap metal and painted wood could all work well.

**Brown-lipped Snail**
This attractive banded snail was found on a shady nettle leaf, and moved to this peeling dead branch in dappled light for a more appealing shot.
*Panasonic DMC-FZ18, ISO 100, 1/250th sec at f4.5*

### Trapping

You can take the uncertainty out of finding invertebrate photographic subjects by setting traps for them. The best kinds of trap are set where the animals are naturally present. One classic is the pitfall trap, which is simply an open-topped container like a tumbler, or flowerpot, sunk into the ground. The idea is that your unsuspecting beetle, woodlouse or centipede is wandering along, doesn't notice the ground has fallen away, drops into the container and is unable to climb out. If you set a pitfall trap, check it frequently, and release any critters that you don't want to photograph. You might inadvertently trap a shrew in one of these – they are about the only mammals short-sighted enough to blunder into one. If you do, release it at once. It's illegal to handle shrews without a licence, and their metabolisms work so fast that even a few minutes without food can have very serious consequences for them.

The strong attraction many moth species have for bright lights has been exploited by entomologists for centuries, and now amateur naturalists can really get in on the act with a light trap. The typical light trap uses a powerful ultraviolet light to draw moths into a box, from which it's very difficult for them to escape. The box is usually stocked with bits of broken-up egg-boxes, giving the moths plenty of easily gripped surfaces to rest on. Prices vary (a lot) according to design, but even the simplest trap will provide you with a wealth of new photographic subjects, probably including species you're unlikely to see any other way. It's normal to set the trap at dusk and empty it at dawn, keeping any specimens you want to photograph for no more than a couple of hours. The best nights for successful moth trapping are warm and still – run your trap regularly from early spring to late autumn to catch a good variety of species.

**Elephant Hawk-moth**
Moth trapping in even the smallest garden or yard can lead to exciting discoveries, such as this Elephant Hawk-moth, in the morning when the trap is emptied. Big moths in particular will usually allow you to gently move them around, so you can place them in a suitable spot for a striking photo.
*Nikon D1X, Nikkor 105mm macro lens, ISO 200, 1/40th sec at f16*

**Grow your own**

You may have reared caterpillars as a child. It's a wonderfully rewarding way to observe nature in action, and at the end of the process you'll have pristine adult butterflies and moths which will hopefully hang around to have their photo taken before they set off to make their own way in the world. If you find some eggs, or caterpillars, and decide to have a go at rearing them, here's what to do.

First of all, make sure you can identify the species – only attempt to rear common species which are on a readily available food plant. Take the eggs/caterpillars home on the plant you found them on (with an extra supply of that plant). Place the plants in water on the ground in your garden (ideally a partly sunny, partly shady spot) with some form of covering over the water so the caterpillars can't fall in and drown. Replace the foliage as required. If you're at all worried the caterpillars are not doing very well, return them to where you found them straight away.

When they are fully grown, the caterpillars lose interest in food and wander off to look for somewhere to pupate. They might attach themselves to a stick or wall for this, or perhaps bury themselves in soft earth. Now you have to wait – the length of time depends on the species so check a reference book. Note that some species over-winter in their pupal form. Hopefully you'll be around on the big day to see the grand unveiling of a shiny new butterfly or moth – the whole process is fascinating, seldom observed and will make for a great set of photographs.

# Handling wild animals

Use both hands to pick up a frog or toad. If you approach it slowly and carefully, it may walk into your hands. If it leaps away before you get near, don't pursue it. If you do catch it, carry it gently in closed hands (so it doesn't jump away, risking injury from a fall). When you want to release it into your set, open your hands slowly – hopefully it will climb out calmly and not immediately dash for cover. When you have finished taking photos, move or gently chivvy your amphibian to a damp, sheltered spot where predators won't see it.

Try to avoid picking up insects and other invertebrates by taking hold of them – their limbs and bodies are fragile, so it's much better to let them walk into your hands, onto a twig or leaf, or into a receptacle of some kind. An obvious exception would be a snail, which you can pick up by its shell (do this slowly if the snail is out and about, giving it time to retract its body into its shell).

Some insects are very lively and liable to dash out of sight the moment they get the chance – to avoid this many photographers place them (inside a container with tiny air holes) in the fridge for a few minutes to slow them down. This probably does little harm to the insect but may increase its risk of being caught by a predator, and chilled insects often look a bit knock-kneed and wear a tell-tale cloak of condensed water droplets. An alternative is to do any insect-manoeuvring early in the morning, when they will be slower because they have yet to warm up naturally – and the light conditions will be appropriate for photos of dew-dusted insects. This is also the best time to move flying insects around – they will often be sleepy enough to let you move them or move the object they're resting on. Learning how to find flying insects at their roosting spots is a challenge but a worthwhile skill to acquire. Using a net to catch larger insects can be literally a hit-and-miss affair – the risk of damaging them is significant and unless you're an experienced netter we can't recommend it.

When you've finished with your subject, you can leave it where it is if the spot is safe and sheltered. Otherwise, return it to where you found it, or to a close approximation of that. Many insects rely on camouflage to protect them from predators while they sleep, so don't leave a dark brown moth perched in full view on a pale green leaf. Place it on a surface that better matches its colour and pattern. If in doubt, conceal your insect in some foliage so it is at least somewhat protected from the gaze of passing birds.

If any mammal or bird allows you to get close enough to touch it, you are almost certainly dealing with either a very young, or a very poorly, creature. If it is the former, take any photos quickly and then leave it alone for its parents to attend to. Only move it if it is in immediate mortal danger, such as being run over, trodden on, eaten by a family pet. If you suspect you've found a sick animal, forget the photos and get in touch with your local wildlife rehabilitator for advice.

**Common Toad**
Although this Common Toad was partly hidden, there was no need to try to move it as the three-way textural contrast between weathered piece of wood, bumpy amphibian skin and lush clover and grass made a pleasing image.
*Panasonic DMC-FZ18, ISO 100, 1/320th sec at f5.6*

# Bringing it together – some examples

Here are some examples of successfully planned and executed photos, with explanations of how and why they were done.

**Garden birds and invisible feeders**

A common scenario – you've got bird feeders and the birds are using them, but you are bored with taking photos of birds sitting on feeders. The feeders themselves aren't that photogenic and because of their design the birds tend to be partly obscured when using them, so the whole thing just doesn't look that 'natural'. The solution is to photograph the birds as they sit on nearby twigs or branches prior to flying to the feeder. Take a little care when siting your bird feeders to

make sure you're going to be able to take shots like this. Try hanging a feeder on a branch with another suitable-looking branch next to it, or set up a cut branch as a perch next to the feeder so that the birds have to land and almost queue before going to the feeder.

**Photo set-up for branch perch** (above)
The simplest set-up possible; a feeder hung on a tree branch with another nearby branch acting as a perch.

**Great Tit on branch set-up** (left)
This photograph was easily taken as the Great Tit waited to fly to the feeder
*Nikon D2X, Sigma 300-800mm lens (at 800mm), ISO 200, 1/160th sec at f5.6*

**Peanuts wedged in tree** (above)
These peanuts have been wedged into an actual tree trunk as opposed to the more common set-up of a fallen branch. Nuthatches and Great Spotted Woodpeckers are frequent visitors to feeders at the same site and it was only a matter of time (and patience on the photographer's part) before the birds found the nuts.

**Nuthatch at nut set-up** (right)
Once this Nuthatch found the peanuts, it was simply a case of waiting for a photogenic pose.
*Nikon D2X, Sigma 300-800mm lens (at 750mm), ISO 200, 1/100th sec at f5.6*

### Goldfinches and Teasels

Once you've accomplished this, you might want to try some more specific bird/vegetation combinations, using baiting. The fat, spiky seed heads of Teasels make appealing photographic subjects. Add a dazzlingly colourful Goldfinch or two and you have the makings of a really pleasing shot – but how to persuade your Goldfinch to sit on your Teasel? As it happens, Goldfinches can, and do, naturally feed on Teasel heads, but if you don't have Teasels growing in your garden, you can fake it. First, though, you need the Goldfinches. If your garden already has them coming to visit, great, if not, you may well be able to attract them if you buy yourself a special bird feeder designed to dispense nyjer seed.

Scatter nyjer seed in the vicinity of the feeder to give them the idea. Goldfinches also like sunflower seeds, so have a suitable seed feeder nearby. Hopefully you'll soon have Goldfinches coming to your feeder. Now, collect yourself some spent Teasels from your local meadow (leave flowering plants alone, take only the dried-up dead ones, and make sure you take a good length of stem too). Fix them in your garden, close to your feeders but in a suitable position for the photo you want (tie them to stakes or to other plants to hold them steady. Shake some nyjer seed into the Teasel heads themselves. Some of it will fall out, but hopefully the Goldfinches will spot the seed that's lodged in between the Teasels' bristles, and will feed on it and give you the photo you want.

**Goldfinch set-up** (left)
Goldfinches will eat standard seed, but love the black nyjer seed shown in the yellow feeder here. If the birds are in the area this seed is virtually guaranteed to attract them to your garden.
*Nikon D2X, Sigma 300-800mm lens (at 300mm), ISO 200, 1/100th sec at f8*

**Goldfinches on nyjer feeder** (opposite)
Once the birds find the feeders they will build in numbers and become regular visitors.
*Nikon D2X, Sigma 300-800mm lens (at 300mm), ISO 200, 1/100th sec at f8*

**Goldfinches on teasel** (left)
Once Goldfinches are regularly visiting, it is a simple matter to remove the feeders on photography days, place Teasels baited with nyjer seed where the feeders used to be and after a short search Goldfinches will land on the Teasels and feed on the seed.
*Nikon D2X, Sigma 300-800mm lens (at 500mm), ISO 200, 1/160th sec at f11*

### Moths on the wall

For those with limited outside space, moths provide some of the best photographic opportunities as they are very responsive to two kinds of attractant – food (in the form of something smelly and sweet) and light. If you leave a window open and a light on for an hour or more after dark, you're likely to attract some moths, especially on warm, still summer nights, and if you're lucky they'll be resting on the wall outside the next morning, although they may well not hang around for long but will go to seek somewhere more sheltered soon after it gets light. By all means attach some vegetation to your wall if you'd like to photograph the moths in a vaguely natural-looking setting, but the plain surface of a painted wall isn't a bad option either as it allows the moths' often beautifully detailed patterning to really stand out.

### Jay feather still lifes

If small-scale photography interests you, it's a good idea to hold onto interesting bits and pieces you may come across in your garden or further afield for use in still-life photography or to 'furnish' sets for shots of small animals. Sometimes your finds will be worthy of centre-stage in your

photos. The black and blue striped feathers from the bend of a Jay's wing are very distinctive as well as colourful. After chancing upon a small clump of them in a patch of woodland, it seemed like a photo opportunity too good an opportunity to miss. Some feathers were collected and taken home for experimentation, trying several shots of them against different backgrounds in an attempt to find complementary shapes and colours.

**Jay feather on Bracken** (above)
A clump of pretty blue wing feathers from a presumably deceased Jay was a lucky find. Hang on to things like this for setting up still-life compositions.
*Panasonic DMC-FZ18, ISO 100, 1/160th sec at f4*

**Jay feathers** (opposite)
*Panasonic DMC-FZ18, ISO 100, 1/250th sec at f4.5*

# Seizing the moment

You've been crouched in your hide since before sunrise, waiting for a Wood Mouse to visit your carefully prepared feeding station. Suddenly there's a commotion at the other end of the garden – you look up just in time to see a Sparrowhawk zipping in to deftly swipe a Great Tit from one of your feeders as the other little birds scatter in panic. The hawk flaps off with its struggling prey. A moment of Attenborough-worthy wildlife drama – and you'd have caught it on camera if only you hadn't had said camera fixed firmly to a tripod with the wrong lens attached.

Wild animals are unpredictable, and inevitably some great photo opportunities happen too suddenly and are over too fast for you to ever stand a chance of grabbing them. However, there are things you can do to improve your chances of being able to react quickly to the unexpected.

**Red Squirrel on feeder** (opposite)
Hanging out feeders in the garden can often turn up surprises, like this Red Squirrel.
*Nikon D300, Sigma 300-800mm lens (at 300mm), ISO 400, 1/25th sec at f5.6*

**House Sparrow** (below)
Sometimes setting up a perch is not necessary. This Pyracantha bush planted alongside feeders in a back yard provides a natural perch for birds landing before feeding. The only frustration is waiting for them to land on a branch that is in the open.
*Nikon D300, Nikkor 300mm lens, ISO 320, 1/200th sec at f5.6*

**Sparrowhawk**
Gardens provide perfect feeding opportunities for a
Sparrowhawk; there is a regular supply of food, usually
throughout the day, and sometimes the other species are so
busy feeding that they are easy targets, like this Starling
was. If feeding birds suddenly scatter in a panic, be ready to
grab your camera.
*Nikon F5, Nikkor 800mm lens, 1/60th sec at f5.6 (original on*
*Fujichrome 100 slide film)*

that there's going to be trouble. Learn the alarm calls
of your local birds (usually a strident repeated note – a
ringing 'chink' or rattling 'tac', but also sometimes a
discreet, thin whistle) and if you hear them, look out
for a predator. Half the time the threat may be
something uninteresting or innocuous – next door's
cat, or your spouse bringing you a cup of tea, but learn
to find the source of the alarm quickly, because one
day it will be something exciting.

**Warning signs**
Hunting animals rely a great
deal on stealth and their
powers of concealment.
However, prey animals are ever alert for signs of
danger, and when they see a predator they often let
each other know in loud, clear and unmistakable tones

**Be aware of the
possibilities**
Knowing the ways of your
local wildlife will help you be
alert to exciting possibilities.
If you've seen urban Red Foxes going in and out of a
possible den locally in early spring, look out for small
cubs having their first outdoor stroll across your lawn

in May. If the local birdwatchers have been reporting an influx of Waxwings in a cold snap, look out for these scarce and stunning birds visiting your berry bushes. After a sudden downpour (especially if it's been dry lately), look out for birds bathing in newly formed puddles. Keep a diary of what you see and when, so that you can predict animal activity in years to come. For example, make a note of when you see your first damselflies, to give yourself a better chance next year of capturing the moment when a damsel nymph climbs out of your pond, then splits down its back to let the brand-new adult insect struggle free.

**Buy more kit**

Having two camera systems ready to go will allow you to switch quickly and easily

**Waxwing**

If you plant berry-bearing shrubs or trees in the garden there is always a chance of species such as the scarce Waxwing visiting in the winter.
*Nikon D2X, Sigma 300-800mm lens (at 600mm), ISO 200, 1/400th sec at f5.6*

from distant-bird to close-up-spider camera and lens arrangements. Of course, what you spend on kit is up to you, and it's very easy to haemorrhage money into your photography hobby, but if you upgrade to a different system, this is one good reason to hang on to your old kit.

# Photo projects

You may find it most fun to point your camera at anything and everything and amass a large and varied collection of photos. On the other hand, you might prefer a more structured approach. Choosing and pursuing some specific photographic projects will help focus your mind and can be a rewarding process which gets you experimenting with ideas you might never have considered. The photos that result are naturally ordered into coherent sets, which you can go on to use or display in other ways (see Chapter 7 for more on this).

Some ideas for photo projects:
• Documenting the seasonal changes in one of your garden trees (the tree itself, the animals that live in the tree, or both)

• A set of close-up, almost abstract images of different tree bark textures
• A collection of standardized comparison photos of all the different little brown moths that come to your garden
• The life cycle of frogs or toads
• An in-depth look at the life of one of your common garden birds
• Experimenting with shutter speeds to capture the shapes and characters of birds in flight
• Building a pond – documenting the stages of its construction and the arrival of new animals
• Giant mini-beasts – perception-jolting eye-level macro images of your garden's creepy-crawlies

## STARLING PROJECT
Photo projects can be great fun to do; they provide a purpose to photography instead of just aimlessly wondering: 'What can I point the camera at today?' In the case of this particular project the idea was to photograph Starlings in different plumage stages, and engaged in different behaviours

**Starlings bathing** (above)
Like all birds Starlings need to bathe and drink, but they are particularly vigorous bathers.
*Nikon D1X, Nikon 800mm lens, ISO 200, 1/320th sec at f8*

**Starling eating berry** (left)
In the autumn Starlings will descend on trees in flocks and quickly clean out the berry supply.
*Nikon D2X, Sigma 300-800mm lens (at 550mm), ISO 200, 1/320th sec at f5.6*

### Starling juvenile (above)

The all-brown plumage of newly fledged young Starlings contrasts strongly with that of the more colourful, glossy-looking adult birds.

*Nikon D300, Sigma 300-800mm lens (at 600mm), ISO 200, 1/250th sec at f5.6*

### Starling flock (top)

Starlings can become very tame if fed regularly, giving the opportunity for a different type of image using a low angle and a wide-angled lens.

*Nikon D2X, Sigma 18-50mm lens (at 40mm), ISO 200, 1/250th sec at f7.1*

### Starling on chimney pot (left)

Starlings will utilize many natural perches to display and sing from; chimney pots are a particular favourite.

*Nikon D1X, Nikon 800mm lens, ISO 200, 1/500th sec at f5.6*

**Starling in winter plumage** (above)
In winter the glossy black, green-hued plumage is covered in white spots, and the bill is dark.
*Nikon D2X, Sigma 300-800mm lens (at 550mm), ISO 200, 1/80th sec at f5.6*

**Juvenile Starling moulting into first winter plumage** (right)
After a couple of months the juveniles begin to moult their feathers, body first, to the spotty winter plumage, resulting in a curious half-and-half appearance.
*Nikon D2X, Sigma 300-800mm (at 800mm), ISO 200, 1/500th sec at f7.1*

**Starling in winter plumage, singing** (opposite)
And so the seasons come around again; this winter-plumaged singing bird has already developed the yellow bill of summer and soon the body moult will begin.
*Nikon D300, Nikon 300mm lens, ISO 800, 1/1000th sec at f6.3*

# 6 Finishing touches

**Great Spotted Woodpecker**

The original version of this Great Spotted Woodpecker shot had the bird facing left and placed more centrally. To make it work better on this page, the bird was cut out, flipped and pasted left of centre, and Photoshop's healing brush was used to iron out the joins – the out-of-focus background made this a fairly simple task.

*Nikon D300, Sigma 300-800mm lens (at 390mm), ISO 320, 1/250th sec at f5.6*

Photography has always been an addictive hobby. With the advent of digital photography, an equally addictive, related hobby has sprung into being – digital image manipulation. All you need is a digital camera, a computer and some modestly priced, or even free, image-manipulation software, and you can enhance, tweak and modify your photographs as much as you like. Not only that, but you can print them out to any size, have them printed onto practically any inanimate object you can think of and publish them online.

# Image manipulation

The term 'airbrushing' has been around for years and originally referred to the use of an actual physical airbrush, to apply a fine spray of ink to a photo, to hide or smooth out imperfections. These days, the word tends to be used to describe digital image alterations of any kind, and it is being overtaken by the term 'photoshopping' after the industry standard software package Adobe Photoshop.

Given that every digital image is composed of pixels, each of which carries a single colour, it's possible to change every detail of any digital picture by changing the colour of some or all of its pixels. In this way you can increase contrast by making the darks darker and the light tones brighter, increase sharpness by giving more contrast to the edges of objects in the image, change colours any way you wish, and replace or duplicate whole sections of the image. However, it is very possible to overdo it and end up with an obviously artificial image. The law of diminishing returns applies as well – sometimes the amount of work required to

**Blue Tit original**
This shot, taken on a gloomy day, is rather 'flat' in tone and colour, and a little soft in terms of focus.
*Panasonic DMC-FZ18, ISO 100, 1/100th sec at f4.2*

**Blue Tit enhanced**
A few quick adjustments to contrast, colour and sharpness help to make the image more appealing.
*Panasonic DMC-FZ18, ISO 100, 1/100th sec at f4.2*

make an image look the way you want it to is so great that you'd be better off just taking another photo. Image manipulation is a powerful tool and it's fun to do as well, but don't rely upon it to make an average photo great – as a general rule think enhancement rather than alteration if you want your photos to look plausibly natural (although by all means have fun experimenting with some more extreme changes too).

## The basics

You can alter an image file in Photoshop, or an equivalent program, in many different ways. You can paint directly onto the image in any colour you wish, using a hard-edged 'pencil', or a 'brush' of any size, shape, softness and opacity. You can fill whole areas of the frame with solid colour using the paint bucket. You can use the eraser to clear pixels. You can use different layers to add overlaid features to your image. You can use any number of special filters to create all manner of optical effects, turning your image into an impressionist painting, a linocut or a photographic negative – the options are endless.

There are often multiple ways to achieve the same goal. For example, to select some pixels so you can work on them without affecting the rest of the image, you can use the magic wand tool (which selects pixels of matching colour), the marquee tools (which let you draw a frame around the area you want to select), the Quick Mask (which lets you paint over the area you want to select with a tool that works like a paintbrush), or by colour or tonal ranges via the Select menu. As you become more experienced with the software, you'll

start to favour certain methods. You will learn a lot through trial and error, and time spent messing around in Photoshop is time well spent for any digital photographer.

We only have space here to look at a few basic tweaks, but once these are mastered you'll find you have the confidence to try other tools and adjustments.

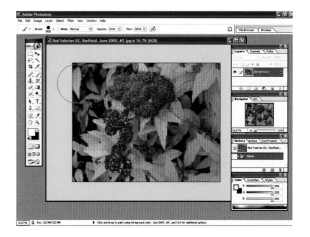

**Photoshop screenshot**
Adobe Photoshop in action. The vertical bar on the left of the screen shows the tools that you can apply directly to the image – the paintbrush for painting on colour, paint bucket for filling in large areas of colour, the magic wand for selecting pixels, the eye-dropper for taking colour samples from the image, the cloning stamp for duplicating areas of pixels and so on. Along the top of the main window are the parameters for the tool currently in use. The four small windows on the right of the screen cover views of levels, channels, a history of actions you've made, a colour swatch chart and so on..

## What software?

Although Photoshop is widely used in commercial publishing, it is rather pricey for the home user. Adobe does a cheaper package for home users – Photoshop Elements – which retains the key functions of its big brother. Both are available for Windows and Mac OS systems. There is also an excellent free open-source package available. The GIMP (Gnu Image Manipulation Program) was originally developed for Linux systems but is now

available for Windows and Mac OS as well. This package, which can be downloaded from the internet, has a similar interface and capabilities to Photoshop.

All of the software packages described above are highly sophisticated and powerful pieces of kit, with more capabilities than you're ever likely to use. There is a range of fat textbooks on the market for anyone who wants to really explore what can be achieved with these products.

## Contrast

One of the simplest and most satisfying tweaks you can make to your images is to bump up the contrast a little. There are various ways to do it, but in a nutshell they work by making the darkest parts of the frame darker, the lightest points lighter, and adjusting everything in between accordingly. The more sophisticated methods involve adjusting 'curves' or 'levels', both of which show you a graph representing the range of tones in the image, and give you precise control over them. Automatic contrast adjustments tend to over-egg the pudding a bit, so experiment with doing it manually. In fact, the same is true of most of the other adjustments you can make to an image.

Improving the contrast gives your image extra clarity and depth, and enhances colours. It works especially well on images taken on overcast days. If you adjust the contrast well, then compare the enhanced image to the original. The original will often appear to have a grey cast over it, as if you're looking at it through a grimy window.

**Thick-legged Flower-beetle original**
It was a dull day but this dramatic green beetle investigating a buttercup was too interesting to ignore.
*Panasonic DMC-FZ18, ISO 100, 1/160th sec at f4.2*

**Thick-legged Flower-beetle with levels adjusted**
Boosting the contrast using levels adjustment has helped to bring out the bright colours.
*Panasonic DMC-FZ18, ISO 100, 1/160th sec at f4.2*

## Channels

All the colours in a digital image are made up of various proportions of the three primary colours of light – red, green and blue (RGB). This will seem counter-intuitive to those of us who know from art lessons that the primary colours are red, blue and yellow, but light behaves differently from the physical pigments in paints or inks. Your downloaded digital image will be displayed in RGB format, but it can be separated into those three individual colour channels. This means that if you want, you can make changes to just the red information in the image, or just the blue or just the green. This could be useful if you want to enhance blues without turning green areas bluish, for example. It also comes into play when making an edge mask (see 'Sharpening' opposite).

If you convert your image to CMYK format (cyan, magenta, yellow and 'key' or black), as you should do before you print it, to see how the colours will look when converted from light to a representation of ink colours, you can make changes to any of those four channels instead.

**Greenfinch, underexposed**

The true colours in this underexposed Greenfinch photo are brought out by use of the levels adjustment and by tweaking the colour balance in the shadows and highlights.
*Nikon D300, Sigma 300-800mm lens (at 440mm), ISO 200, 1/320h sec f5.6*

**Greenfinch, after adjustment**

## Colours

Often, improving the contrast in your image is enough to enhance the colours sufficiently. If you want to make further improvements, one option is to increase the saturation. Applied to the whole image, this makes every pixel a more intense tone of the colour it already is. A light hand is essential when increasing saturation, as over-saturated images can be quite scarily vivid and very unnatural-looking.

You may want to just change some of the colours in the image and leave others as they are. You can do this by selecting only the one channel you want to work on, by manually selecting (clicking on) the parts of the image you want to change using the magic wand tool, or by using the command 'select colour range'. You can also adjust the colour balance of all or part of the image – increasing the proportion of blues will make your image look 'cooler', while red will warm it up.

## Sharpening

Once you start experimenting with sharpening, you'll quickly realize the limits of image-manipulation software. You can't turn a blurry image into a crystal-clear sharp one because the software can't add missing information – it can only make an educated guess. If sharpness is your aim, make sure you achieve it when you press the shutter, because you won't be able to do much about it at the computer.

It is, however, possible for sharpness to be improved to a certain extent. The various kinds of sharpening work by looking for areas of contrast in the image, and making that contrast more pronounced by brightening the lighter pixels and darkening the darker ones. Therefore, if you plan to sharpen an image and improve its contrast, do the contrast adjustment first so the sharpening has more clearly defined edges to work on. Taken too far, sharpening will turn all the edges in your image to jagged black and white lines, so as ever go easy.

You can 'spot-sharpen' points on the image using the sharpen tool, which works like a brush tool. There is also a general sharpening filter. However, the most powerful sharpening method is the confusingly named 'unsharp mask', which allows precise control of the amount of sharpening applied.

# Sharpening your images

One of the main problems with any kind of sharpening is the creation of artefacts. Say your photo has an area of clear blue sky. The sharpening tool will inevitably find spots of contrast in that area which are too subtle to stand out to our eyes. However, once these slight contrasts become sharpened, they become visible, as spots or speckles. The problem can be avoided to a certain extent by using 'sharpen edges' rather than 'sharpen', but this too can be a bit hit and miss.

The method below uses the example of a Starling

**Starling original**

It's worth taking a little extra time to sharpen up a slightly soft image, like this Starling photo, exactly the way you want it, rather than applying a general sharpening filter and hoping for the best. In this case, an edge mask was used to select the areas to which sharpening should be applied.
*Panasonic DMC-FZ18, ISO 100, 1/200th sec at f4.5*

**2]** On the copied channel, apply the 'Find Edges' filter. This will produce a white image with edges shown as black lines.

**3]** Invert the image so the edges become white lines against a black background

**1]** Look at the three channels, one at a time, on their own. Choose the one that shows the best contrast, and make a copy of it. View just this new channel for steps 2-5.

image and describes how to make an edge mask (i.e. to block off part of the image) which will protect everything except the edges of the image, so that sharpening can be applied here only and not to the areas of flat colour.

**6]** Now view the image as a whole once again. Your selection will still be marked.

**4]** Now tidy, expand and soften the edges – apply Median filter to take away odd speckles (radius 1-2 pixels), then Maximum filter to expand the edges (radius 2-4 pixels), then Gaussian Blur to soften the edges (radius 2-4 pixels)..

**7]** Apply Unsharp Mask. Set the amount to anything between 50 and 150 (higher number for a larger image), the pixels to 1 and the threshold to zero.

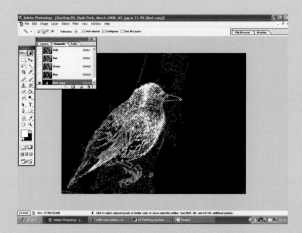

**Starling with sharpened edges**

**5]** Use the magic wand tool to select the edges. Set its tolerance to about 15 pixels. Make sure it is in 'add' mode rather than 'replace' or 'subtract' so that you can select all the areas you want to. Leave out any erroneous areas of edge, such as in areas of sky.

**Chaffinch with intrusive twig**

That blurry twig coming out of the bottom left of the frame and poking the Chaffinch in the ribs rather spoiled this photo. It was removed using the cloning tool and healing brush, in a rather ambitious bit of digital manipulation that involved reconstructing bits of branch, background and Chaffinch. It's worked out quite well, but bear in mind that the simpler the removal job, the better the result is likely to be.
*Panasonic DMC-FZ18, ISO 100, 1/50th sec at f4.2*

## Removing unwanted elements

Here's one adjustment that you may already have in mind when you're taking the photograph. Let's say you've just lined up a great shot of a Blackbird on your lawn. The sun's shining, the light's just right, the pose is there… everything's perfect – apart from an old bus ticket someone has thoughtfully thrown over the fence into your garden and, more importantly, into your photograph. Even in your own private outdoor space you can't always guarantee the absence of distracting elements in the frames of your photos, but don't let this stop you pressing the shutter, as it's often possible to remove them from the image later on. Even if you never want to carry out any image manipulation, it's still worth learning how to do these techniques, as you can use them to remove any speckles on your image caused by dust specks on your camera's sensor.

The two most widely used 'replacement' tools are the cloning stamp and the healing brush. Both work like other 'brush' tools, so you can vary the size and opacity of the brush you use. The former lets you copy pixels and 'paint' them elsewhere. The latter does essentially the same thing but with more 'intelligence' – it looks at the surrounding pixels and tries to blend everything together smoothly. To get rid of an element, find an adjacent area of suitable pixels from which to

**Chaffinch with twig removed**

copy, hold down 'alt' and click on that area, then release 'alt' and carefully paint over the undesired pixels. It takes practice to get a tidy finish, and it is much easier on uncluttered backgrounds. Cloning out an aeroplane from a clear blue sky is very simple, cloning out a particular twig from a muddled tangle of other twigs much less so.

If you want to cover over a large area of pixels, you can select an area of suitable replacement pictures using one of the marquee tools (either the preset shape marquee or the lasso), copy the area selected, then paste it down and move it to where you want. Doing this will create a new layer, so you'll then need to flatten the image to restore it to one layer, and possibly tidy up the edges of the pasted-on pixels using the cloning stamp or healing brush.

**Softening the background** A variation on replacing distracting bits and bobs is to soften the whole background of your photo to make your subject stand out more clearly. The same method is used to create 'cut-outs'. This is tricky and often time-consuming to get right, and won't work well on every photo, so don't expect the earth. What you need to do is to select your subject, then invert your selection so that everything but your subject is selected. Probably the easiest way is to use a Quick Mask. Clicking this creates a new layer. When you paint onto it, wherever you paint becomes masked off from the rest of the image (and shows up as a single-coloured semi-opaque highlight – pinkish-red in Photoshop). Paint over your whole subject, and anything else in the frame that connects directly to your subject (for example the twig a bird is perched on) with a soft brush. Be extremely careful at the edges – use the eraser to rub out any mistakes. Now click the magic wand tool

**Great Tit**

The maze of twigs surrounding this Great Tit was a little distracting. By selecting them in sections and applying a Gaussian blur, their intrusive presence was reduced.
*Panasonic DMC-FZ18, ISO 100, 1/250th sec at f4.5*

**Rabbit original**

This is a decent shot of a backlit baby Rabbit, but it could be better framed. Using the crop tool, a couple of alternatives were quickly created.
*Panasonic DMC-FZ18, ISO 100, 1/250th sec at f5.6*

**Great Tit with blurred background**

in the unmasked parts of the image to select them. To blur the background, apply a Gaussian Blur to the unmasked areas. To make a cut-out, simply clear or erase the unmasked areas.

**Rabbit, horizontal crop**

**Rabbit, vertical crop**

### Cropping

Ideally, you have framed your image perfectly when you pressed the shutter, and the composition is beyond reproach. In real life, we can't all be superstars all of the time, and often a little judicious trimming at the edges can improve the composition of a photograph. The best reasons to crop are probably to make your subject larger in the frame, to cut out distracting and/or irrelevant areas, and to move the subject off-centre for a more pleasing composition. Cropping will reduce the overall image size – something to bear in mind if you plan to enlarge or print out the photo.

# Printing

If you like photo albums, you probably appreciate the most significant advantage of conventional film cameras over digital – with film it was always very easy to get your mitts on a shiny set of prints. With digital images, sorting out the photos you want printed, and then either printing them yourself or having a professional do it is more of a chore than dropping a roll of film and a cheque into a prepaid envelope and posting it.

Most modern inkjet printers can print out photos to a high standard, provided you use decent photo paper (which is readily available in the standard print sizes). However, they can be very ink-hungry, and some models are prone to jamming, getting clogged up with ink or otherwise breaking down. It's worth paying a bit extra for a reliable and economical printer if you'll be printing a lot of your own images. By choosing the professional option you'll usually pay a rate per image, and you'll need to provide the printer with a CD, DVD or memory stick with your images on it.

### Preparing your images for print

Remember the difference between RGB colour and CMYK colour? It's important to change your images from RGB mode to CMYK mode before you print, as this will show you an accurate representation of what they will look like when printed. The difference is quite often very slight, maybe even too slight to notice. Where you are most likely to see a difference is in images that have areas of very pure red, green and (especially) blue. Blue skies that look dazzling in RGB can become a little muddy-looking in CMYK because ink colours can never be as pure as the colours in light, although the software will do its best to get a very close match.

The default image file type on most systems is JPG (jpeg), which is a compressed image type, ideal if you are storing lots of photos or sending them by email. For printing, you may see better quality if you convert your JPEGs to uncompressed TIFF files.

You should also check that the image size and resolution are right before you print. If you are shooting your photos in a high-quality mode, the

## Resizing images

When you look at the image size information, you'll see a 'document size' (in inches or centimetres) and a resolution (number of pixels per inch or per centimetre). These factors determine how big the individual pixels are, and therefore how smooth the image looks. Images with relatively fewer, larger pixels (low-resolution or 'low-res' images) will look blocky and jagged, especially at points of contrast. The higher the resolution, the smaller the pixels are and the smoother the image looks.

To change the picture's size without affecting the overall number of pixels in the image, the proportions or the size of the file in terms of data, you'll need to make sure the 'resample image' box is not ticked, and that the 'constrain proportions' box is. If you change one of the image dimensions, the other will change automatically to keep the proportions, and the resolution will change too, to ensure that the overall number of pixels in the image doesn't change – instead, the pixels themselves change size. If you change the resolution, the image dimensions will change accordingly.

Say you have an image that is 3,264 pixels across and 2,448 pixels deep. At 72 dpi its dimensions will be 115.15 x 86.36 cm. Changing the resolution to 300 dpi will bring its dimensions down to a more manageable 27.34 x 20.73 cm. If you then want to print it out at 16 x 12 cm, you can either change the dimensions again in the same way and print it at 518.16 dpi, or check the 'resample image' box then change the dimensions to what you require. This will constrain the resolution to 300 dpi while changing the dimensions, and therefore reduce the number of pixels in the image to 1,890 cm across and 1,417 cm deep.

finished images may well be too large for conventional photo print sizes.

For an image to look good in print, you'll need a resolution of at least 300 pixels per inch (dpi) or 118 pixels per centimetre. If your printer can only print 600 dpi, an image of 1200 dpi printed out on it won't look any better than a 600 dpi image, so don't assume a higher dpi always produces a better-looking picture.

## Printing your images onto other things

You might not be able to run a mug through your home inkjet printer, but print studios can put your images onto all kinds of things. If you're sufficiently proud of your photos to give them to friends and family as gifts, you can have them printed onto placemats, crockery, canvases or fabrics, sets of playing cards and so on.

# Desktop publishing

Ever wanted to see your name and your photos in print? There are numerous photo magazines out there that will consider ideas for written articles illustrated with your own photos – if you feel you have the gift of the gab, why not share what you've learned and what you've achieved and try sending off a few submissions.

Alternatively, you could design and print your own material. Word processing programs like Microsoft Word or its free open-source equivalent OpenOffice Word Processor (NeoOffice on the Mac) allow you to combine words and pictures, while dedicated desktop publishing software like Adobe InDesign are more powerful and sophisticated page design options. You could save money and impress friends at the same time by making your own greetings cards (use your photo-editing software to paint Santa hats on your Robins if you wish!), or make printed materials for your own reference – an identification chart of your garden's wild flowers, moths or birds perhaps.

**Redwing card**
Save money (well, some money) on Christmas cards and show off your work at the same time by printing appropriately wintery photos onto greetings cards and adding a seasonal greeting.

# Publishing online

If you're using a digital camera you've already embraced the technology zeitgeist, so there's no sensible reason not to start showing off your photos on the Internet. A quick surf around will reveal any number of amateur photographers' websites and blogs, and it really is the easiest way to showcase your work for anyone – people you know and people you don't – to view and enjoy.

**Websites** To have your own dedicated website, built and designed to your exact requirements, you will need to register a domain name, and you'll need to find a web-hosting company that will 'hold' your web pages for you on a network of dedicated computers (servers). Many web hosts will handle the domain name registration for you. The registration and hosting will cost you a few pounds (usually in the region of £5-£15) each month. (You may be able to get a free domain name if you don't mind having some third-party advertising on your site.)

Once you've set this infrastructure in place, you need to build your site – or pay someone else to build it for you. With a bit of technical savvy and the use of website-building software like Dreamweaver or any number of free open-source programs, you should be able to make a functional and attractive site, but if you know a tame web designer, now's the time to call in any favours they might owe you. If neither of the above applies, you can pay a professional to design your site for you – but if you do get help, try to make sure that they show you how to update the site yourself. You don't want to have to phone up someone every time you want to add a new photo to the site.

Whether you go it alone or have some (or a lot of) help, you'll find it useful to consider how you want the site to look and to function, what your introductory or home page should look like, how you want your images to be organized

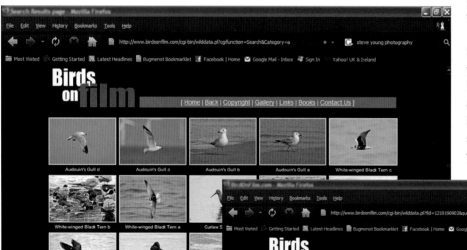

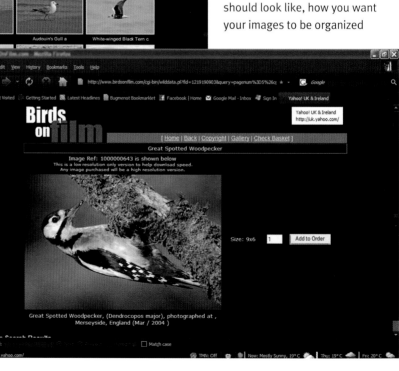

**Steve Young's website**
Professional wildlife photographers like Steve Young can show off and sell their photos online via a website. The images are divided into themed galleries, and the thumbnail photos can be clicked to view full-size versions.

and so on. Sketching out screenshots is a good plan for working this out. Be mindful that large images take longer to load than small ones, especially on slower Internet connections – and web surfers have very short attention spans. Using thumbnails that click through to full-size images is a good plan, so visitors can select the photos they want to view. Images don't need to have resolution higher than 72 dpi to look good on screen.

## Blogs

A truncation of 'web log', the blog or online diary is a popular and simple way to give yourself an online presence for free, and a well thought-out blog will do just as well as a full-blown website for many amateur photographers. To start a blog, go to a blogging website like www.blogger.com and follow the instructions. You won't have much control over how your blog looks, but you will be able to upload your photos as well as any text you want to include. Blogs probably work best if treated as they were intended to be used – as online diaries. A blog is perfect for keeping an illustrated record of the wildlife in your garden and your photographic exploits.

## Protecting your copyright

Here's something that's a worry for anyone who publishes their work online. You automatically own the copyright on all your photographs, but that fact may not deter people from copying your images without your permission, and perhaps making use of them in some other media, or even claiming them as their own. You can help prevent this by registering your images with the copyright registration service, by pasting a '©John Bloggs' label onto each image, by watermarking (embedding copyright information within the digital file itself using special software) or by any combination of these three methods. The UK Copyright Service has all the information you need.

## Hotlinking

Lots of people don't realize that 'hotlinking' (directly linking) images from one website to another is a definite no-no. If Bob decides to link one of Andy's online images into his own blog or website and you view that that image on Bob's site, you will be doing so via Andy's web host's servers, not Bob's. When you view a web page, you are using that

**Sample blog**
Free and easy, blogging is the quickest way to get your photos online.

site's bandwidth (its capacity to transfer data) to display the files. Since web hosts charge based on the amount of data transferred, Bob's hotlinking increases Andy's bandwidth consumption, and therefore potentially also his monthly bill. The practice is sometimes called 'bandwidth theft'. Avoid doing it yourself, and discourage people from doing it to you – it's a good idea to post a 'no hotlinking please' request on your site or blog.

## What next?

If you get bitten by the photo bug, then exciting times are ahead. Even the biggest and best garden on Earth has its limits, and you'll soon be champing at the bit to point your camera at a more diverse array of life on Earth. The UK is replete with nature reserves that often have excellent resources for photographers and almost guaranteed sightings of otherwise hard-to-see animals. Head abroad and the possibilities multiply still further – you might need to pay a surcharge for lots of camera-related luggage but you won't regret it when you're photographing Leopards in Botswana or albatrosses in New Zealand. If travel's not for you, just get exploring in your local countryside – you never know what you will find. The skills you've honed photographing the wildlife in your garden will serve you well in the wider world, and it's not a one-way street – your efforts to make your garden a hospitable place for wildlife will help to really enhance the richness of your local environment.

# Further information

## Useful websites

The web is awash with handy stuff and also with misinformation. The selection of sites below includes those specifically mentioned in the book, as well as other reliable and useful resources.

### Computers and software

UK Copyright Service www.copyrightservice.co.uk
Everything you need to know about your copyright (including online copyright) and how to protect it.

The GIMP www.gimp.org
Download a powerful – and free – open-source image-manipulation software package here.

Picasa http://picasa.google.com
A free, Google-developed program that helps you organize your photos, as well as carry out simple image improvements.

Blogger www.blogger.com
A popular free blogging site.

OpenOffice www.openoffice.org
From here you can download a free open-source suite of office software, analogous to Microsoft Office.

UK Web Host Directory http://uk.webhostdir.com
Lists UK-based web hosts. Includes useful information on choosing a host, and a handy discussion forum.

Free Web Hosts www.free-webhosts.com
A directory of companies offering free web hosting.

### Wildlife information and advice

The Mammal Society www.abdn.ac.uk/mammal
Stacks of information on the UK's mammals.

The Royal Society for the Protection of Birds (RSPB) www.rspb.org.uk
Has lots of help on attracting birds to your garden.

The Wildlife Trusts www.wildlifetrusts.org
Plenty of advice and links to county wildlife trusts.

Reptiles and Amphibians of the UK www.herpetofauna.co.uk
Exhaustive site about UK reptiles and amphibians.

UK Butterflies www.ukbutterflies.co.uk
A guide to all the UK butterflies – how to identify them, what their habitat requirements are, and when and where you'll see them.

UK Moths http://ukmoths.org.uk
As above, but deals with the UK's 2,000-odd moth species.

UK Safari www.uksafari.com
A general site celebrating the UK's wildlife, with identification galleries for many plant and animal groups.

Wild About Britain www.wildaboutbritain.co.uk
Another general wildlife site (including plants), with galleries, information and a wide variety of very active discussion forums.

RSPB Land Management Courses
www.rspb.org.uk/ourwork/conservation/advice/training/habitattraining.asp
Find out about the RSPB's various training courses on managing land for conservation.

### Shopping – wildlife

RSPB Shop http://shopping.rspb.org.uk
Stocks a range of birdfood, feeders and nestboxes, as well as things to attract other wildlife to your garden.

CJ Wildbird Foods www.birdfood.co.uk
Sells all kinds of bird food, feeders, nest boxes and wildlife gardening accessories.

Garden Bird Supplies www.gardenbird.com
Offers a huge selection of food, feeders and other items.

NHBS Environment Bookstore www.nhbs.com
Has thousands of wildlife books available.

WildSounds www.wildsounds.com
Full selection of audio and multimedia guides and books.

Wildlife Watching Supplies www.wildlifewatchingsupplies.co.uk
Sells hides, shelters, camouflage materials, ground sheets and other handy kit for photography.

Alana Ecology www.alanaecology.com
Moth traps, bat detectors, hand lenses and other essentials for the naturalist.

Really Wild Flowers www.reallywildflowers.co.uk/
Online shop selling native wild seeds, bulbs and shrubs.

Tree2MyDoor www.tree2mydoor.com
Buy native tree saplings for your garden.

## Shopping – cameras and camera kit

Nikon www.nikon.co.uk
Canon www.canon.co.uk
Olympus www.olympus.co.uk
Pentax www.pentax.co.uk
Fujifilm www.fujifilm.co.uk
Panasonic www.panasonic.co.uk
Sony www.sony.co.uk
Sigma www.sigma-imaging-uk.com
Tamron www.tamron.com

Websites for the leading digital camera manufacturers and (Sigma and Tamron) makers of SLR lenses. Check the company websites for the 'last word' on specifications.

Trusted Reviews www.trustedreviews.com
UK-based, independent and detailed reviews of digital cameras (and other kit and gadgets).

Jessops www.jessops.com
UK-wide high street retailer of cameras and kit.

In Focus www.at-infocus.co.uk
Optics (including cameras and digiscoping kit) for wildlife watchers and photographers. Holds outdoor events at nature reserves so you can test kit in the field.

London Camera Exchange www.lcegroup.co.uk
Buy new and second-hand camera kit and optics by mail order or in store.

# Recommended reading

You could easily fill a fair-sized library with useful books on wildlife, gardening, photography and photo editing. The following is a small selection of the best.

## Computing

Beginning GIMP Learning from novice to professional level, by Akkana Peck (Apress).

Photoshop CS3 for Dummies by Peter Bauer (John Wiley and Sons).

Photoshop Elements 6 for Dummies by Barbara Obermeier and Ted Padova (John Wiley and Sons).

The Really, Really, Really Easy Step-by-step Guide to Building Your Own Website by Gavin Hoole and Cheryl Smith (New Holland).

## Wildlife

Attracting Birds to your Garden by Stephen Moss and David Cottridge (New Holland).

Attracting Wildlife to Your Garden by John A. Burton, David Tipling (New Holland).

Bill Oddie's Birds of Britain and Ireland by Bill Oddie (New Holland).

Collins Complete Guide to British Wildlife: A Photographic Guide to Every Common Species by Paul Sterry (Collins).

Complete Garden Bird Book by Mark Golley, Stephen Moss and David Daly (New Holland).

Complete Garden Wildlife Book by Mark Golley (New Holland).

Cooking for Birds by Mark Golley (New Holland).

Garden Bird Year by Roy Beddard (New Holland).

Gardenwatch by Sarah Whittley (New Holland).

Green Guides: Garden Wildlife of Britain and Europe by Bob Gibbons (New Holland).

Secret Lives of Garden Wildlife by Dominic Couzens and Peter Partington (Christopher Helm).

Ultimate Birdfeeder Handbook by John A. Burton and Steve Young (New Holland).

Wildlife Trusts Guide to Garden Wildlife by Nicholas Hammond (New Holland).

## Gardening

Organic Gardening Techniques by Nick Hamilton (New Holland).

Starting out with Native Plants by Charlotte De La Bedoyere (New Holland).

Weekend DIY: Garden Ponds by Bryan Hirst (New Holland).

## Photography

Complete Digital Photography by Tom Ang (New Holland).

RSPB Guide to Digital Wildlife Photography by David Tipling (Christopher Helm).

Photography Handbook by Sue Hillyard (New Holland).

Really Really Really Easy Step-by-Step Digital Photography by Gavin Hoole and Cheryl Smith (New Holland).

# Glossary

This is a quick-reference guide to technical words and phrases. Note that some of them are explained in more detail within the relevant part of the book.

**Airbrushing** Smoothing out imperfections in digital images.

**Ambient light** The available light in a scene, whether natural or artificial.

**Aperture** The hole that lets light through to the camera's sensor when the shutter is pressed.

**Apochromatic (APO) lens** A lens corrected for colour abnormalities in all three primary colours, to control chromatic aberration.

**Artefact** An unwanted piece of digital 'misinformation' in an image.

**Aspect ratio** The ratio of width to height in an image.

**Centre-weighted metering** A light metering system that reads the light mostly from the central portion of the viewfinder.

**Chromatic aberration** Colour 'fringing' around the edges of elements in an image, which is the result of a lens struggling to focus on different colours on the same focal plane.

**Compact camera** A small camera with a built-in lens.

**Compact flash card** A type of memory card for storing digital images and other data.

**Compression** A way of making a digital file smaller (taking up less memory space) by removing redundant information. Over-compression starts to remove important visual information and causes the image quality to degrade.

**Converter or teleconverter** A supplementary lens that can increase the length of a telephoto lens.

**Cropping** Printing or using only part of the original image, by digitally 'cutting out' a section from the frame.

**CMYK** The four colours used in colour printing: cyan, magenta, yellow and black.

**Depth of field** The distance between the nearest and furthest objects in sharp focus in a photograph.

**EXIF data** Information stored with a digital image, including camera type and exposure settings.

**Exposure compensation** A camera setting that allows you to deliberately over- or under-expose an image to allow for particular light or contrast.

**Extension tubes** Metal tubes between the lens and body of SLR cameras, to extend the lens film distance for taking close-up photos.

**f-number or f-stop** The number that indicates the size of the lens opening.

**Feeder** A container designed for dispensing food for birds or other animals.

**Fill-in flash** A flash used to soften or 'fill in' the shadows caused by bright sunlight.

**Focal length** Determines the magnification at which a lens 'sees' distant objects.

**Hide** A permanent shelter that conceals the photographer from the wildlife.

**JPEG** A compressed image file format, the default file type on most cameras.

**Lens** The (built-in, or removable) tube on the front of the camera, which contains sheets of glass to focus and magnify the image.

**Lens flare** Spots of bright light on an image, caused by reflections inside the lens when light shines directly on it.

**Lens hood** A metal or plastic tube that prevents unwanted light from falling on the lens surface and causing lens flare.

**Macro lens** A lens that can focus on very close objects.

**Megapixel** A million pixels. A '10-megapixel' camera can store images containing 10 million pixels.

**Metering** The way the camera assesses the amount of available light when deciding how best to expose an image.

**Mirror lens** A telephoto lens that uses mirrors to shorten the path of the light through the lens, so that the lens can be physically smaller.

**Native** Indigenous to a given area. The House Sparrow is native to the UK, the Canada Goose is not.

**Overexposure** When too much light reaches the sensor, producing a bleached-out image.

**Panning** Following a moving subject with the camera, producing a blurred background.

**Photoshopping** Any kind of digital alterations.

**Pixel** The individual squares of colour that make up a digital image.

**RAW file** An unprocessed digital file direct from the camera, which must be opened and adjusted with specialist software.

**Resolution** The number of dots (pixels) per inch in a digital image.

**RGB** Red, green and blue – the primary colours of light as recorded in digital imaging.

**Saturation** The intensity and richness of colours in an image.

**Sensor** The device in the camera that receives the image and converts it into digital information.

**Sharpening** Digitally increasing edge contrast and therefore apparent sharpness.

**Shutter** The button that opens the aperture to take a photograph.

**Shutter speed** The length of time the aperture is open when the shutter is pressed.

**SLR** A larger camera with interchangeable lenses.

**Spot-metering** A light metering system that reads the light from a very small portion of the viewfinder.

**Telephoto lens** A lens that magnifies the image, allowing you to take frame-filling photos of distant objects.

**TIFF** A high-quality, uncompressed file format widely used in digital photography.

**Underexposure** When insufficient light reaches the sensor, producing an image that's too dark.

**White balance** The relative amounts of red, green and blue light in an image.

**Wide-angle lens** A short focal length lens that 'sees' a greater angle of view than a standard lens.

**Zoom lens** A lens that allows a variable focal length.

# Index

Page numbers in bold refer to picture captions